GUARDIAN
OF THE FLAME

ART OF SRI LANKA

FIRST EDITION, 2003

CATALOGUE SPONSORS:

Northern Trust Bank,

Dr. Sukumar Nagendran,

Dr. & Mrs. Quintus Fernando,

M. Phelps, Calvin Eng,

James & Sharon Bourg.

DESIGN AND PRODUCTION:

Agency: Crosby-Wright

Creative Director: Jeffrey Moss

Designer: Lisa Quirin-Hand

Scottsdale, Arizona

www.crosby-wright.com

PUBLISHED BY:

Phoenix Art Museum

1625 N. Central Avenue

Phoenix, AZ 85004-1685

Published in conjuction

with the exhibition

Guardian of the Flame:

Art of Sri Lanka

February 8 – May 11, 2003.

PHOTOGRAPHY:

Unless otherwise noted, all photography

is by John Hall Photography.

Phoenix, Arizona

www.johnhallphotography.com

ISBN# 0-910407-50-9

© 2003 Phoenix Art Museum

All rights reserved.

FRONT COVER:

Buddha
Kandyan Period: 18th Century
Gilt Bronze
H 66cm W 22cm D 22cm

TABLE OF CONTENTS

Foreword

Janet Baker, Curator of Asian Art—Phoenix Art Museum

As the twenty-first century world grows smaller and becomes more interconnected, it seems that the number of remote and mysterious places to which few have traveled is diminishing. Yet there are still some names that evoke a sense of the unknown, the unspoiled and the unexplored. Perhaps Sri Lanka is still among them. As an island nation, it has retained its distinct identity over the centuries, allowing Buddhist art, philosophy and culture to remain alive and changing. Few museums outside Sri Lanka have significant collections of Sri Lankan art. A small number of collectors have pursued its treasures. Thus, Phoenix Art Museum is honored to have the opportunity to present to its audience an exhibition of Sri Lankan art spanning two millennia, drawn entirely from private collections that have never before been on public view.

Guardian of the Flame: Art of Sri Lanka allows us to learn about an artistic tradition that is almost entirely Buddhist. Through the objects in this exhibition, we can better understand how the profound truths taught by Sakyamuni Buddha over twenty-five hundred years ago became manifest in exquisite works created out of bronze, wood, ivory, crystal and stone. Through the various essays, both scholarly and personal, in this publication, one can explore the significance of the Buddha's message to humanity, that of wisdom and compassion as the path to spiritual enlightenment. The passion expressed in these writings is strong evidence for its relevance and timelessness.

Every exhibition and publication comes to fruition through the efforts of a dedicated team of players. In this case, I would like to extend heartfelt thanks on behalf of Phoenix Art Museum to Northern Trust Bank, Dr. & Mrs. Quintus Fernando, M. Phelps, Calvin Eng, James & Sharon Bourg, Dr. Sukumar Nagendran, Valerie Crosby and Jeffrey Moss at Crosby-Wright Advertising & Design, Lisa Quirin-Hand, John Hall Photography, and the Museum's Asian Arts Council and Men's Arts Council for their generous support. I applaud the talented contributions of Dr. John Listopad, Michael Phillips, Victoria Chan-Palay, Sherry Montgomery and Thuy Tran for making this publication a rich and varied perspective on art history, religion and collecting. I am most grateful for the unwavering support of Jim Ballinger, Director of Phoenix Art Museum, for our ongoing programs of Asian art. Though anonymous, the collectors of Sri Lankan art who have allowed their rare treasures to be on view deserve our recognition for their unselfish kindness and dedication to the appreciation of art and culture. Their generosity is truly in the Buddhist spirit of purity, nobility and beauty as embodied in these marvelous works of art themselves.

Janet Baker, Ph.D., is Curator of Asian Art at Phoenix Art Museum. She is a specialist in Chinese Buddhist art and archaeology, and has published numerous books and articles on the subject. Prior to her appointment at Phoenix Art Museum, she was at the Bowers Museum of Cultural Art in Santa Ana, CA and at the China Institute in New York.

Acknowledgements
HOMAGE TO THE LINEAGE OF TEACHERS

John Listopad—Stanford University

These essays are not intended to illustrate the entire development of Sri Lankan art, but rather to examine it through a few select objects from this exhibition. As a result, some very important trends and developments are absent or barely touched upon. One omission of note is the rise of Mahayana Buddhism in Sri Lanka and the complex and refined arts associated with it. While of great importance to the development of Sri Lankan art history, there are few unquestionably Mahayana objects in the exhibition and it was impossible to treat it with the consideration that it deserves within the scope of this catalogue.

I would like to thank Roland De Silva who provided invaluable assistance during my fieldwork in Sri Lanka so many years ago, and the late Professor Joti Kaliyanamitra of Silpakorn University, Thailand with whom I had the privilege of visiting Sri Lanka and who encouraged me to return and continue my studies. Over the years Professor Lennox Tierney of the University of Utah, Professor Walter Spink of the University of Michigan, Ann Arbor, and the late Professor Howard Wilson of Capital University have guided my studies and provided sage counsel and advice. Special thanks to the collectors who graciously made their collections available to me for study. And lastly, I would like to express my deepest gratitude to Dr. Janet Baker for inviting me to collaborate with her on this project.

The monumental work of Ulrich von Schroeder in *Buddhist Sculptures of Sri Lanka* has been an invaluable reference. Never before have so many photographs of Sri Lankan sculptures been assembled and competently organized in conjunction with important primary reference material. His insightful comments and his subsequent *The Golden Age of Sculpture in Sri Lanka* were particularly inspirational.

The essay on the development of style through the Anuradhapura period is largely based on the work of Douglas Barrett and Diran Kavork Dohanian. Ananda Coomaraswamy and Richard Gombrich provided the source material upon which the description of the consecration of a Buddha image is based. The section on the *Sariputra* is derived from the work of Ananda Coomaraswamy and Hans Ruelius, while the essay on the cult of relics owes a great deal to the work of Senarat Paranavitana and C. E. Godakumbara.

A COLLECTOR'S PERSPECTIVE

Though works from their collections are not part of this exhibition
and publication, these two collector's reflections on Southeast Asian art
reveal the passion and dedication of their pursuit.

The Art Lover as Collector

Victoria Chan-Palay— New York

Art collecting is a passionate sport. All collectors are avid hunters of the objects of their heart's desire. Almost all these objects would undoubtedly be considered works of art by their owners or their would-be owners. An object can be as simple as an unusual sea-shell on the beach found by an observant child, or a unique sculpture produced by a craftsman in a community inhabiting the Eurasian steppes many centuries ago. Both of these examples have in common, an inherent value and beauty in the eye of their beholders. So personal and so overwhelming might be the drive and passion for the article in question that its collector may consider it a simple accident that an external market value is placed upon it. Monetary values placed on objects of one's passionate desire may be so entwined with the passion that the collector

is inured to price, perhaps explaining some of the extravagant dollar values placed on many art objects in recent times.

Every object can undoubtedly be attached to a story or a memory, as with any tale of passionate love. All such stories have a beginning and an end. It might be a tale of love at first sight, a slow waltz, a sprint, or a long marathon run towards the acquisition of the actual object. It may have been driven by passion or perhaps by cool intellect. The object may be just a passing fancy, or it may be a piece destined for an enduring love through the life of its owner. In most cases, the falling in love with an object of art for a true collector invariably leads to the physical possession of the object. If it is part of a continuing process of aesthetic development, then the new possession is likely added with fanfare and pride to a collection. This collection of objects may stay within a modest total number, or the new object may join a veritable army of like or related objects.

The items in a collection may be proudly displayed and admired by the collector and by others who appreciate them or learn to cherish them with like reverence. Or, the collection may be carefully hidden away to be savored only in secret by its owner who is jealous of sharing its beauties and mysteries with other presumed possessive eyes. The display of these articles can be purely private in well-protected sanctuaries of a personal home or space, or the location chosen for a collection may be very public, to be visited by as many interested viewers as possible.

Collectible objects can belong to a special area so unusual or new as not to have been heretofore recognized. It can occupy a small niche in a much larger, recognized field that has perhaps escaped the attention of other active collectors. This would make it easier to find appropriate collectible objects that, because they are less sought-after simply by being lesser known, can be bought at a lesser price. In other cases, price itself may prove no deterrent. Stories abound of collectors who dive directly into the most populated areas of collecting fearlessly, valiantly in search of objects for their collections at any cost. However that may be, it is certainly true that every collector has his or her story about how that favorite masterpiece of the collection was discovered and captured for an unbelievably small price. We all love to possess a treasured piece at a bargain price, even if we have lost our hearts despite its cost.

The fields of collecting that involve art from contemporary artists have the advantage that their sources and authenticity can be more readily validated. Those that encompass objects from ancient eras and distant and exotic lands require great expertise in sources and authentication on issues of repair, reconstruction and records in order to meet the highest standards. Knowledge of every aspect of an object may not be too much to ask of one who aspires to be a great collector. Renowned collections are formed by those collectors who have had the great luck to come upon extraordinary objects under auspicious conditions and with superb advice. Such collection are never born; they have always been made at great cost and tremendous drive, determination and energy, with an overriding interest in the subject.

Finally, the daunting task of forming a wonderful collection of art objects is never finished. There is the constant work of sorting out those objects that hold one's aesthetic attention from those that no longer do, of culling in order to meet and perchance to surpass the highest of standards set by the world's great museums. The final result might become that stellar collection of several masterpieces of unsurpassed beauty and rarity amongst a supporting cast of other pieces that enlarge our knowledge of and appreciation for that field of art. This is the end to which we all strive.

Biography

Victoria Chan-Palay, M.D., PhD., DSc., has been widely honored for her academic achievements, medical research and accomplishments as teacher, writer, artist and scholar. She has held high academic and clinical positions on three continents and senior executive positions in the pharmaceutical industry. In the public sector, she has served as White House Fellow to the Secretary of Defense at the Pentagon. As a young athlete, she represented her native Singapore in international swimming competitions. She was the first woman to receive the M.D. degree with highest honors at Harvard Medical School and has received the Alexander von Humboldt Prize for medical research from Germany. She has won numerous other prizes for her work on disease mechanisms in the brain, and is a world authority on Alzheimer's disease. As founder of the leading international journal *Dementia and other Geriatric Cognitive Disorders,* she continues as editor-in-chief, has authored five books, numerous articles, and book chapters, and she speaks several languages, including German and Chinese. Dr. Chan-Palay has been included in the *Esquire* magazine register of "The Best of the New Generation: Men and Women who are Changing America," "Remarkable Women: A Smith Continuum," and has been called a true renaissance woman. She is a distinguished collector of ancient Southeast Asian art.

B.A. Smith College

M.D. Harvard Medical School

Ph.D. Tufts University School of Medicine

D.Sc. (honorary) Smith College

Buddha Amitabha
Michael Phillips Collection
Central Java, Indonesia: 8th–9th Century
Andesite Volcanic Rock
H 113cm

Reflections in a Mirror

Michael Phillips—Los Angeles

Is amassing a collection of Buddhist art the very antithesis of the Buddhist teachings of non-attachment and letting go? Maybe not.

While wandering through a Fifth Avenue bookstore in 1975 my eye fell upon the oddly titled *Tibetan Book of The Dead*. Wondering what it could be, I reached high to retrieve it and unknowingly took the first step in my great, secret, internal adventure.

After absorbing what I could through reading about Buddhism, I found that I was ultimately too much of a Westerner to make much progress, and I began looking into the art as a way of deepening my experience. I found it calming and compelling at the same time. Encountering a great Buddhist work creates for me an envelope of silence, where time has stopped. This may be the closest I will ever get to experiencing the blissful state described in the teachings, but for me, it is enough. When Buddhist sculpture moves me through its beauty and spiritual force, it works like a tuning fork. Those noble qualities expressed in the piece begin to resonate within me. When I feel connected in that way, I can use the piece as an aid in meditation, and I can contemplate what it must feel like to wear such an expression on one's face. Maybe I can build a better "me".

I plunged into collecting. At first, I wanted one of everything—a Buddha from each classical culture—a carryover from my days of collecting baseball cards. I wound up with fifty small bronzes lined up like toy soldiers in my bookcase. There was pleasure in filling the gaps and expanding my knowledge, but only a few of the objects gave me that feeling which drew me to the art in the first place. I began to wonder what was driving my collecting urge, and if there was any plan at all.

Fortunately, or unfortunately, within the arena of collecting lurk all of the demons that Buddha instructed us to do battle with: Competition, Ego, Greed, Acquisitiveness, Envy, Pride and even something akin to Lust. But amidst the din is the voice of the heart responding to beauty as it nourishes the spirit. How does one act amid this cacophony? By listening. My favorite objects spoke to me from the moment I saw them. When I enter the room my eye invariably goes first to them. I force myself to make appointments to spend time with my other objects, the assorted bargains, "important" pieces and rarities, but somehow, my eyes long to return to those I bought for beauty. Those I bought by listening to the demons are painful and expensive lessons that I am always glad to get rid of.

On a more earthly plane, I have found the process of collecting to be enormously stimulating. As I study the Buddha image and its cross-cultural evolution, I find the joy of discovery, of making connections, and of sharing insights and questions with others in the field. There is a creative and intellectual satisfaction, as key building blocks are found and put into place, transforming a group of objects into a coherent illustration of a central quest.

I recognize the fundamental irony in being a collector within a tradition whose essential teaching is that non-attachment is the path to liberation, but my goal in this lifetime is to learn and to expand my awareness, and to understand myself and my thought processes so that I can make wise choices. These are also Buddhist values.

Collecting Buddhist art has been a wonderfully rich journey for me, an adventure, a fascinating geographic, historical and philosophical tour, an education in how these marvelous works in stone and bronze are made, and much more. I have met knowledgeable collectors, dealers, curators, conservators, scholars and historians who inevitably open my eyes, enabling me to see something in a piece that I have not seen before. I have enjoyed the thrill of the hunt, finding things I never thought I would find. And I have made choices. Along the way I have learned a lot about myself, warts and all.

BIOGRAPHY

During his career in film Michael Phillips has produced thirteen feature films, two television films, and forty-one half-hour television episodes. His films have been nominated for a total of twenty-three academy awards. His personal awards include the Best Picture Oscar for producing THE STING, for which he also subsequently received the Producer's Guild of America's Hall of Fame Award; the Palm D'Or for winning the Cannes Film Festival as producer of TAXI DRIVER; and the David Donatello Award (Italy's Best Picture "Oscar") for producing CLOSE ENCOUNTERS OF THE THIRD KIND. Among his other films are THE FLAMINGO KID (Award of Merit from the Academy of Family Films), CANNERY ROW, DON'T TELL MOM THE BABYSITTER'S DEAD and MIMIC. He most recently served as executive producer of IMPOSTOR, released in January 2002.

Mr. Phillips is a graduate of Dartmouth College and New York University School of Law, was admitted to the New York State Bar, and worked for two years as a Wall Street financial analyst. He has been collecting Asian art for almost thirty years.

Images of Sri Lanka

On landing in Ceylon by air one is miraculously immersed in glistening palms, emerald waters and shadowed jungles, the air is perfumed by a mixture of temple flowers, saffron and coconut oil. You can set off along any one of five different roads, through forests of teak, eucalyptus, rubber and jak trees, or through fields of pine-apple, rice, tobacco and sugar cane. But it would be both foolish and foolhardy to proceed at anything but a leisurely pace—the scenery is too spectacular, the hazards are too great. The Island has the appearance of a gay village fair—on every hand you encounter bare-chested men in multi-coloured sarongs, women in saris which compete with the rainbow, naked children, bicycles, bullock carts, Buddhist monks swathed in togas of primrose, yellow and saffron, even hibiscus-crimson, with lacquer begging bowls and palm-leaf fans, and of course elephants large and small carrying logs, bundles of sugar cane, or just uprooting tropical philodendron and ferns…miniature, yes, the Island is, in contrast to it's great northern neighbor, but the visual range, like it's topography, is infinite…

Roloff Benny
From "Island Ceylon"
1970

Paddy Field on the Road to Mihintale

© 2002 C. B. Amb

▲ *Ruvanvelisiya Dagoba—Anuradhapura*

Moment of Reflection ▶

▲ Detail of Stairway—Anuradhapura

◄ Guardstone—Anuradhapura

▲ *Standing Buddha—Gadaladeniya Vihara*

Young Buddhist Monk—Colombo ▶

© 2002 C. B. Amb

THE CULT
OF RELICS

Aerial View of the Thuparama and Ruvanveliseya Dagobas

The Cult of Relics:
RELIQUARIES FROM THE EARLY ANURADHAPURA PERIOD
(C. 269 B.C. — 3RD CENTURY A.D.)

John Listopad—Stanford University

Almost all objects worshiped by Theravada Buddhists are literally "reminders of the Buddha," *Buddhacaitya*.[1] These are divided into four groups that are defined by their relationship to the historical Buddha. The first and most important class of objects for veneration is the physical relics of the Buddha. Both the actual remains and any architectural monument that contains them are called *dhatucaitya*.[2] Examples of this class of objects include the Buddha's collarbone that was enshrined by Devanampiyatissa (c. 250-210 B.C.) in the first historical *dagaba (stupa)* built in Sri Lanka, the Relic of the Buddha's Tooth at Kandy, and footprints of the Buddha, such as the famous footprint on top of Adam's Peak in south-central Sri Lanka.

Next in importance are objects that were used by the Buddha, such as his alms bowl, or are associated with different events in his life, including the Bodhi Tree, his footprints, and the first Buddha image made during his life. These are called "reminders by association," *paribhogacaitya*. The teachings of the Buddha, such as the Pali Canon

or a commentary on it, are called "doctrinal reminders," *dhammacaitya*. Lastly, there are objects that function as "indicative reminders or symbols," *uddesikacaitya*. Examples of this type of object are the places associated with events in the Buddha's life, copies of famous relics of the Buddha or *dagabas* containing relics, copies of *dhatucaitya*, copies of footprints of the Buddha, and Buddha images, copies of *paribhogacaitya*.

The cult of relics played an important role in Sinhalese kingship. After embracing the Buddhist doctrine and donating monasteries to the Buddhist missionaries, the first devotional act of King Devanampiyatissa was to build the Thuparama *dagaba* to enshrine the collar-bone of the Buddha, a corporal relic or *dhatucaitya*, and another *dagaba* to enshrine an object that the Buddha used, a *paribhogacaitya*, his begging-bowl. Implicit in the accounts of Devanampiyatissa's reign is that he was a universal monarch, a king among kings, as the relics would only come to the land of a universal monarch who supported the Buddhist order. Succeeding

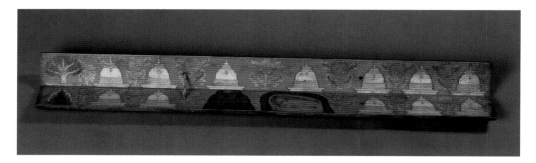

Manuscript Cover
Kandyan Period: 19th Century
Wood with Paint Detail
H 63cm W 6cm
IMAGE 1

kings participated in elaborate annual and semi-annual ceremonies honoring the relics and the Buddhist order. The last large-scale *dagaba* to be made during the Anuradhapura period was that of the Jetevana Vihara, by King Mahasena (c.274-301). While succeeding kings would enlarge and enhance existing *dagabas*, only one other monumental *dagaba* was begun at Polonnaruva, under King Parakramabahu I (1153-1186), and it was never finished.

After the construction of the Jetevana, a shift occurred away from the cult of the *dagaba* to the cult of relics that were physically in the care of kings and were never enshrined in a *dagaba*, such as the Tooth Relic. Despite this, the great *dagabas* remained important pilgrimage sites and were depicted in paintings on temple walls and on manuscript covers through the Kandyan period (IMAGE 1). This pair of manuscript covers portrays sixteen of the most famous pilgrimage sites in Sri Lanka; thirteen of the sites depicted are *dagabas*.[3]

Today, the palladium of Sri Lanka is the Tooth Relic that, according to tradition, was brought to Sri Lanka from the northeast Indian kingdom of Kalinga during the reign of King Sirimeghavanna (c. 301-328). It has been kept in a special room of the Dalada Maligava at Kandy since 1592, enshrined inside multiple gem-set gold reliquary containers, *karanduvas*, in the form of *dagabas*. Since its arrival in Sri Lanka during the fourth century, it has been considered to be one of the most important symbols of

Sinhalese kingship. Its importance to royal legitimacy is most clearly presented in the account of the reign of King Sri Vijaya Rajasinha (1739-1747). Born a Tamil Prince, and a practicing Hindu, he assumed the throne on the death of his brother. As a Buddhist king he was expected to ensure that the Tooth Relic was properly housed, and he built a new temple for it. There was opposition to his rule among the Sinhalese nobility; he was told that a calamity would occur if he were to personally move the Tooth Relic to a new temple, despite the tradition that only a king could move it. Accordingly, he left the matter to the Sinhalese nobles and temple caretakers who found that they could not open the *karanduva* to transfer the relic. On hearing this, Sri Vijaya Rajasinha returned to Kandy were he was able immediately to open the *karanduva* and all of the other caskets inside without difficulty, thereby confirming his right to rule.[4]

Each Sinhalese *dagaba* usually had three relic or shrine chambers, one above another, embedded deep in brick masonry. They were never intended to be seen after they were sealed and the *dagaba* built around them. In addition to being repositories for relics of the Buddha or an eminent monk, these chambers were often elaborately painted and were an integral part of the cosmological symbolism embodied in the architecture of a Sinhalese *dagaba*. In this relic chamber from an 8th-century *stupa* near the Kantaka Caitya at Mihintale, the square dolomite column in the center symbolizes the mythical Mount Meru that stands at the center of the traditional Sinhalese Buddhist universe (IMAGE 2). On top of it was a miniature gold reliquary,

Relic Chamber from a Stupa near the Kantaka "Caitya" at Mihintale
Anuradhapura Period: 8th Century
Anuradhapura Museum—Sri Lanka
IMAGE 2

Reliquaries
Anuradhapura Period: 2nd–4th Century
Crystal
H 6-8.3cm W 3–4cm
IMAGE 3

karanduva, in the shape of a *stupa*. The paintings on the walls depict the guardians of the four directions, *lokapalas*, and celestial beings.

The relics were commonly enshrined in successive gold or crystal *karanduvas* that were often placed within a stone casket (IMAGES 3 & 4). The early Anuradhapura-period *karanduva* made in the form of a *dagaba* from dolomite marble has on its interior a recess in the form of a six-pointed star carved into a lotus blossom that would have held a crystal or gold reliquary. (IMAGES 5a & 5b) The shape of the dome, *anda*, of these reliquaries associates them with the early Anuradhapura period. At that time *dagabas* and *karanduvas* in the form of *dagabas* were made with domes in the form of an almost perfect half circle.

Reliquary Casket
Anuradhapura Period: 2nd–4th Century
Dolomite
H 30.5cm W 30.5cm D 23.5cm
IMAGE 4

According to the *Mahavamsa*, this shape originated when King Dhutthagamani wished to build the first of the great *dagabas* at Anuradhapura, the Ruanvali Caitya. The king asked an architect:

"In what form wilt thou make the caitya?" At that moment Vissamkama (the architect of the gods) entered into (and possessed) him (the architect). When the master-builder had had a golden bowl filled with water, he took water in his hand and let it fall on the surface of the water. A great bubble rose up like unto a half-globe of crystal. He said: "Thus will I make it."[5]

During the Polonnaruva and succeeding periods, the proportions of the bell, *anda*, of the *dagaba* changed from that of the simple half dome of the early Anuradhapura period. The *anda* became higher and narrower as can be seen in this example from a *dagaba* associated with King Parakramabahu I. (IMAGE 6) The bronze reliquary here might have been made for the ashes of a respected monk and almost certainly had other, smaller *karanduva* set inside it.

During the Kandyan period, ivory relic containers became more common (IMAGE 7).

Reliquary
Anuradhapura Period: 2nd–4th Century
Dolomite
H 20cm W 20cm D 20cm
IMAGE 5a

Interior of Dolomite Reliquary
With six pointed star carved into a lotus blossom.
IMAGE 5b

Made by the caste of ivory turners, as opposed to the caste of ivory carvers who worked on Buddhist sculptures, the form of its *anda* is similar to that of *karanduva* from the Polonnaruva period. It has been simply decorated in a restrained manner with colored lacquer. This ivory *karanduva* might have been used to hold the ashes of a lay person prior to their final disposition.

END NOTES

1 While usually used by Western scholars to refer to an architectural monument, the word *caitya* has the broader meaning of "any reminder."

2 They are also referred to as *sariradhatu*, though this classification also includes the remains of disciples of the Buddha and universal monarchs, *cakkavattin*.

3 The sites depicted are:
  A The Mahiyangana *dagabas* encased within each other
  B Nagadipa *dagaba*
  C Kalaniya *dagaba*
  D Samanakuta, The Buddha's Footprint on Adam's Peak
  E Divaguha, the *parinibbana* of the Buddha
  F Dighavapi *dagaba*
  G Mutiyagana *dagaba* (in Badulla)
  H Tissamahavihara *dagaba* (in Rohana)
  I The Bodhi Tree
  J Maricavatti-*caitya*
  K Ratanavaluka *dagaba* (Mahathupa at the Mahavihara)
  L Thuparama *dagaba*
  M Abhayagiri *dagaba*
  N Jetavana *dagaba*
  O Selacetiya
  P Kajaragama (in Rohana)

4 *Chulavamsa*, Vol. 2, 248-249.

5 *Mahavamsa*, 199.

Reliquary
Polonnaruva Period: 12th Century
Bronze
H 52cm W 32cm D 32cm
IMAGE 6

Reliquary
Kandyan Period: 19th Century
Ivory and Lacquer
H 11cm W 3cm D 3cm
IMAGE 7

Reliquary
Polonnaruva Period: 12th Century
Bronze
H 61cm   W 41cm   D 41cm

Reliquary
Late Polonnaruva Period or Early Divided Kingdoms Period: 12th–14th Century
Bronze
H 21cm W 12.5cm D 12.5cm

BIOGRAPHY

John Listopad, received his B.A. in the Visual Arts from the University of California, San Diego in 1973, followed in 1983 by an M.A. in the History of Art from the University of Utah. In 1995 he received his Ph.D. in the History of Art from the University of Michigan, Ann Arbor, on the completion of a dissertation demonstrating the interplay of European, Japanese, Persian and Thai artistic influences at the court of the 17th-century Thai King Narai. From 1995 to 2000, he was the curator primarily responsible for Himalayan and Southeast Asian Art at the Los Angeles County Museum of Art. Since October 2000, he has been the Patrick J.J. Maveety Curator of Asian Art at the Iris & R. Gerald Cantor Center for the Visual Arts at Stanford University.

Dr. John Listopad has spent many years studying in Asia in such diverse areas as working with a Japanese swordsmith, six years in fieldwork in Thailand, as well as visiting remote monasteries in Ladakh. The development of Sri Lankan art has been one of his primary fields of interest, especially the ways in which it has influenced the development of Southeast Asian art and religion.

THE CULT
OF THE BUDDHA
IMAGE

Seated Buddha
Kandyan Period: 18th Century
Gilt Bronze (Eyes inset with blue hardstones)
H 28cm W 23cm D 10cm

The Cult of the Buddha Image
MANUFACTURE AND CONSECRATION

John Listopad—Stanford University

Every Sri Lankan Buddhist temple has a shrine that usually contains several, but at least one, Buddha images. Virtually every Sri Lankan Buddhist household has an altar in front of a statue of the Buddha. According to tradition, all Sri Lankan Buddha images are meant to function as reminders of the Buddha and his teachings, *uddesikacetiya*. As the 17th-century traveler to Sri Lanka Robert Knox (1641-1720) noted: *"As for these Images they say they do not own them to be Gods themselves but only Figures, representing their Gods to their memories; and as such they give them honor and worship."* [1]

There is no evidence of any Buddha image that has an uncontested date before the first century A.D. All traditions concerning an image of the Buddha made during his life must be considered stories created to provide a lineage for a specific Buddha image. One of the oldest descriptions of the physical appearance of the Buddha appears in the *Lakkana Sutta* of the *Digha Nikaya* that is part of the orthodox Pali Canon. In this text the Buddha is described as having the thirty-two marks, *laksana*, of the "Great or Universal Man," *mahapurusa*. This provided artists with a symbolic description of the Buddha. All of these characteristics can be seen on different images in this exhibition. With the exception of the swirl of hair between the eyebrows, *urna*, almost all of these features are found on Sri Lankan Buddha images of all periods. Beginning in the Period of Divided Kingdoms and through the Kandyan period, the *urna* also became a standard feature. Some of the most noticeable marks are:

"1. He has feet with level tread...2. Designs of wheels on the soles of his feet... 3. He has projecting heels...4. He is long in the fingers and the toes...9. Standing without bending he can touch his knees with either hand...11. His complexion is bronze, the color of gold...14. Every hair of it, blue black in color, curling to the right... 19. The length of his body is equal to the compass of his arms...31. Between the eyebrows appears a hair mole, white and

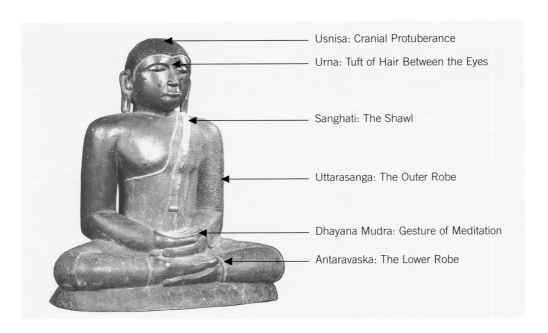

Usnisa: Cranial Protuberance
Urna: Tuft of Hair Between the Eyes

Sanghati: The Shawl

Uttarasanga: The Outer Robe

Dhayana Mudra: Gesture of Meditation
Antaravaska: The Lower Robe

Iconography of Sri Lankan Seated Buddha Images
FIGURE 1

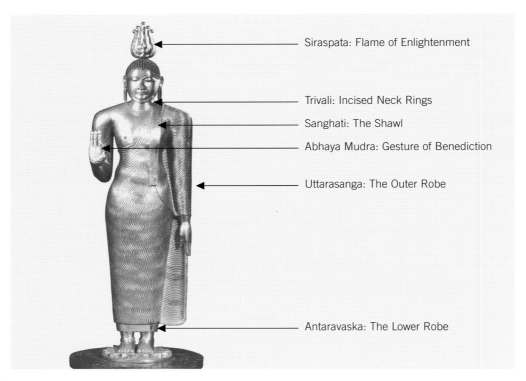

Siraspata: Flame of Enlightenment

Trivali: Incised Neck Rings
Sanghati: The Shawl
Abhaya Mudra: Gesture of Benediction

Uttarasanga: The Outer Robe

Antaravaska: The Lower Robe

Iconography of Sri Lankan Standing Buddha Images
FIGURE 2

like soft cotton down (urna)…*32. His head is like a royal turban (usnisa)…*"[2]

Sri Lankan artists also followed iconometric texts that described in minute detail the proportions of every part of each type of image. One of the earliest Sinhalese texts to have survived is the *Sariputra*. It is believed to have been composed during the 12th-century by a monk named Sariputra. The name Sariputra is a common name, however, and it is impossible to determine who the actual author was. The author of the *Sariputra* used the breadth of a finger to define the basic unit of measurement for each type of Buddha image in the course of 139 verses. This basic unit determined the proportions of the face; the size of the face was used to define the proportions of the other parts of the body. For both paintings and sculptures, the artist would draw a grid based upon the proper proportions. The following verses from the first part of the *Sariputra* give an idea of the guidance that was available to artists:

"*Listen, in the following I will teach the proportions of the Buddha image…in whichever of the three types that it may be made, sitting, standing, or lying, and from whatever material that one makes a statue, be it gold, copper and clay, stone, wood, bricks or lime-plaster, the proportions should be those described below…*

All the proportions should correspond to each other in the following ways and be synchronized with one another as described in the following: the proportions of a image should be determined according to the size of the shrine and the size of a shrine according to the size the image. Proportions other than those arrived at by these two methods are not sanctioned…

The actual measures of the stature are derived by this means, that one its breadth and length must respectfully be determined by the use of use of a real finger's breadth as a unit of measure. Once the actual measures of the length and breadth are determined, the measurement of the breadth of the shoulders can be determined…

The wise man makes an image according to the size of the fingers' breadth of the donor or of others or according to the size of the shrine. (An image is to be proportioned either according to the size of the donor or of the shrine. If you are wise, you will work according to the proportions thus arrived at and applied.)

I will teach the theory of the measurements of the body of a statue of the Buddha. When measured by the breadth of a finger according to the highest module-ten system the length of the body is 124.

One part measures two double fingers' breadths and a half, fingers the length breadth of the face measures 13-1/2 fingers' breadths. From the sole of the foot to the crown of the head will measure nine face lengths and one part.

According to all systems of proportions the length of the face is three parts. The Usnisa measures eight barleycorns from the crown of the head and the height of the hair is three fingerbreadths.[2]

From the hair to the line of the eyes, from the line of the eyes to the lower edge of the side of the nose, to the chin measures at any given point is one part. For the hollow of the chin use the thickness of a half finger breadth."[3]

Once the physical proportions of a Buddha image were established, the garments, postures and gestures were determined

by fixed iconographic conventions. All Sri Lankan Buddha images wear the three robes of a Buddhist monk: the outer-robe, *uttarasanga*, the lower robe, *antaravasaka*, and the shawl, the *sanghati* (FIGURES 1 & 2). Unlike Buddha images from other Buddhist countries, Sri Lankan Buddha images are usually depicted in just two postures, seated and standing. When they are seated, they are invariably seated in the posture known as *virasana*, where one foot rests on the ground and the other leg is folded so that its foot rests on the calf of the other leg. Standing images are invariably depicted frontally with both feet side by side.

Both seated and standing Sri Lankan Buddha images often have at least one of their hands raised in a symbolic gesture, the most common of which are:

1. The gesture symbolizing benediction through removing fear, *abhaya mudra*. This is usually made with the right hand. The hand is raised to shoulder height with arm crooked and the palm of the hand facing outwards. When the palm of the hand is turned to the image's left, the gesture is called *asis mudra*, a variant form of *abhaya*

mudra[4]. The most famous Sri Lankan Buddha image making this gesture is the monumental image at Avukana.

2. The gesture symbolizing offering, charity, and compassion, *varada mudra*. This can be made with either hand. The arm is lowered with the hand open and the palm facing out.

3. The gesture symbolizing elucidation, discussion, or argument, *vitarka (vyakhyana) mudra*. Again, this gesture can be made with either hand. It is made by having the thumb and forefinger touch.

4. The gesture of meditation or *samadhi, dhyana mudra*. The left hand rests palm up on the lap, the right hand is placed palm up on top of it.

Sri Lankan artists used the lost wax or *cire perdue* method to cast images. The image would be modeled in wax by the sculptor. If a hollow image was desired, the wax image was built up over a clay core and iron wires were used to keep the core in place during firing. Wax flues for the venting of air and other gasses during casting were attached at strategic places, and the whole was encased in a fine mud or plaster. It was then baked in a fire to burn out the wax, leaving a hollow. A molten copper alloy would be poured into the mold and allowed to cool. The mold was broken away, the casting flues were cut off, and any flaws in the surface were filled, usually using a soft copper alloy. As most images in Sri Lanka were cast using brass, they usually had fewer surface flaws and required less infill than those cast in bronze. The surface was polished and surface details were incised. If those commissioning the image were generous enough, the final step prior to consecration might be mercury fire-gilding.

While small images were usually solid-cast during the early Anuradhapura period (c. 200-432), large images were usually hollow-cast. During the late Anuradhapura period, images of all sizes were usually solid-cast. The most likely reason for this change in practice is the influence of the South Indian Hindu *silpasastra* tradition, which strictly forbids the making of hollow images of deities for worship.[5] This is different from the practice in North Indian Hindu and Buddhist religious art where numerous large images were hollow-cast. By the time the

Sariputra was written, the casting of solid images in Sri Lanka was codified and the making of hollow images was explicitly forbidden:

"Whether one will make a portable or stationary statue, those who would attain illumination, let none of them, whether they are working in gold, iron, or any other material, a statue with a hollow body.

When anyone makes a statue with a hollow body, they will set in motion strife and the loss of their possessions and all that is good. Not long after, a famine will break out, trade and commerce will come to a halt, and the king will be deposed." [6]

After a Buddha image was completed, no matter in what medium it was made, it was consecrated through an elaborate ritual. At the center of the consecration ceremony was the ceremonial "opening of the eyes." This was accomplished either by inlaying eyes on the face of the image, engraving or carving the eyes, or painting the eyes. Robert Knox noted in the 17th century:

"Some being devoutly disposed, will make the image of this God (Buddha) at their own charge...Before the eyes are made, it is not accounted a God, but a lump of ordinary Metal, and thrown about the shop with no more regard than any thing else. But when the eyes are to be made, the Artificer is to have a good gratification, besides the first agreed upon reward. The Eyes being formed, it is thenceforward a God. And then, being brought with honor from the Workman's Shop, it is dedicated by Solemnities and Sacrifices, and carried with great state into its shrine or little house, which is before built and prepared for it." [7]

The consecration ceremony is today formally called "the meritorious action of establishing the eyes," *netra pinkama*, and is accompanied by the "festival of setting the eyes," *netra pratisthapana utsavaya*. [8] According to the *Mahavamsa*, the Emperor Asoka first performed the "feast of the eyes" when the serpent king Mahakala magically created an image of the Buddha from his memory. [9]

The eyes of the most important stone images during the Anuradhapura and Polonnaruva periods were made of crystal and precious stones that were laid into the eye sockets as part of the consecration ceremony (IMAGES 1 & 2). There was also an annual ritual in which the eyes of an image would be removed, cleaned and replaced, as is noted in an inscription from the Atadage at Polonnaruva: *"...the Hall of Fragrance for the auspicious and colossal stone statue of the Holy Buddha, in which is held annually the ceremony of the unloosening of the eyes (of the image) and applying collyrium to them."*[10] During the Kandyan period the *netra pinkama* ceremony was performed each time a temple was established or refurbished, as all of the Buddha images would need to have their eyes painted and be re-consecrated.

The procedures for the consecration of images was well documented in artists' and architects' guidebooks such as the *Vidyavastu Sastra* which describes a ceremony for consecrating a Buddha image that is similar to that used today.[11] Present practice usually involves having an image's eyes painted by the craftsman who made it. Today, these craftsmen belong to the *sittaru* sub-caste of smiths, *navandanno*. They are skilled craftsmen who are primarily painters, but who also work in metal, stone,

Dolomite Head of the Buddha
Late Anuradhapura Period
With hollow worked eyes originally inset with rock crystal or precious stones.
IMAGE 1

© 2002 John Listopad

Crystal Eye
Late Anuradhapura Period: 12th Century
IMAGE 2

ivory and lacquer. An auspicious day is chosen according to the lunar calendar when an asterism of the moon, *nekata*, occurs at around 5 to 6 a.m. As the Buddha is believed to have attained enlightenment at 5 a.m., the eyes should ideally be painted at this time, though in practice the time varies. Much of the ritual surrounding the painting of the eyes involves the propitiation of various deities to ward off evil images. The ceremonies that the craftsman performs address the Hindu gods that have been adopted into the Sri Lankan Buddhist pantheon, including Indra, Brahma, Vishnu, Siva, Ganesa, as well as the planetary deities. The last altar visited is to Ganesa, the Lord of Obstacles, a shrine to whom is often found at both Hindu and Buddhist temples in Sri Lanka (IMAGE 3). At around 5 a.m., the craftsman and an assistant are locked alone in the temple; it is not opened until the ceremony is complete. The craftsman looks over his back to a mirror in order to paint in the eyes; he does not gaze directly at the image. Even so, after completing the ceremony his gaze is considered dangerous and he is lead away from the temple blindfolded, along with a pot into which all of the evil that has accumulated during the ceremony has been channeled. At the proper spot, the blindfold is removed from the eyes of the craftsman. His gaze falls on a tree, water basin, or similar object that functions as a scapegoat; he breaks the pot against it and then symbolically slays the scapegoat with a sword. While Buddhists in all countries consecrate Buddha images by painting or engraving the eyes, this elaborate ritual with its emphasis on warding off ill-fortune is uniquely Sri Lankan.[12]

Ganesa
Jaffna Period: 19th Century
Bronze
H 23cm W 11cm D 10cm
IMAGE 3

END NOTES

1 Robert Knox, *An Historical Relation of Ceylon,* reprint of 1681 edition (Glasgow: University Press, 1911), 116.

2 *Lakkana Sutta* of the *Digha Nikaya* iii, 1, 142 ff.

3 Hans Ruelius, *Sariputra und Alekhyalaksana,* (Gottingen: Dissertation Georg-August Universitat, 1974), 120-3.

4 While a 3rd-century early Kushan period Buddha image from Mathura displays *asisa mudra,* it did not become popular in Indian Buddhist sculpture. In Sri Lanka it was used on the monumental standing Buddha at Avakana, and as this image was widely copied, it has become part of Sri Lankan Buddhist iconography.

5 The *Sariputra* did permit less important images that would not be used for worship to be hollow cast.

6 Ibid., 123.

7 Robert Knox, 130-131.

8 Most of this description of the ceremony of the "opening of the eyes" is derived from Richard Gombrich's description in "The Consecration of a Buddha Image," *Journal of Asian Studies,* Vol. XXVI (1996), No. 1, pp 23-36. Ananda Coomaraswamy described the consecration of a monastery and its Buddha images during the Kandyan period in his *Medieval Sinhalese Art,* first ed. 1908.

9 Mahavamsa, 33-34.

10 Epigraphia Zeylanica Vol. II (1912-1927) ed. *Don Martin de Zilva Wikremasinghe,* reprint of 1928 ed., (Colombo, Government Press, 1985), 254. This is a posthumous inscription honoring Vijayabahu I (1116-1137) composed by the South Indian mercenary troops, Velaikkaras, to whom he entrusted the care of the temple of the Tooth Relic at Polonnaruva.

11 The *Vastuvidya Sastra* ascribed to Manjusri, E. W. Marasinghe trans., (Delhi, Sri Satguru Publications, 1989). vol. 2, 149–183.

12 Hindu images are consecrated with a very similar ceremony, using a mirror, and it is very likely that this particular ceremony was adapted from Hindu practice. A plate full of sweets is placed in front of a Hindu image so that it will be the first thing that the image's eyes see. Great care is taken to avoid having the image's first gaze fall upon the person opening the eyes. Sinclair Stevenson, *The Rites of the Twice-Born,* reprint of the 1920 edition, (Delhi: Oriental Books Reprint Corporation, 1971), 413-414.

THE ART OF
SRI LANKA

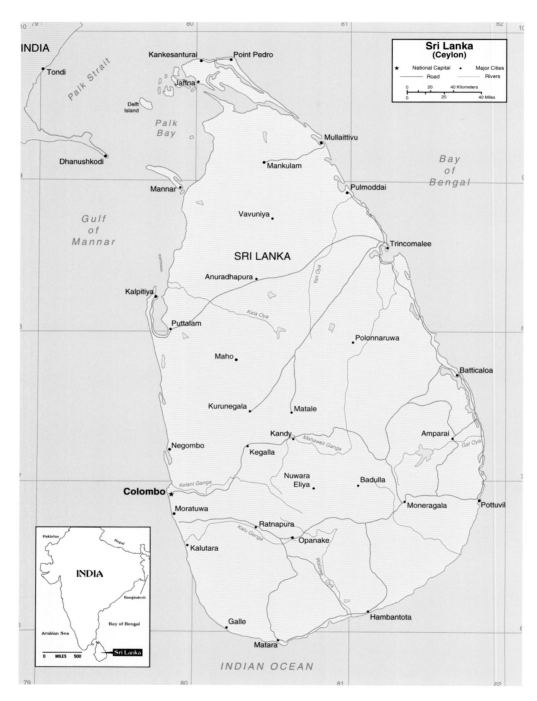

Sri Lanka

The Art of Sri Lanka:
THE HISTORICAL CONTEXT

John Listopad—Stanford University

Sri Lanka is an island nation measuring approximately 430 kilometers from north to south and 225 kilometers from east to west. It is separated from the southeast coast of India by the Gulf of Mannar, which at the narrowest point is just 34 kilometers across. Its close proximity to India has meant that it has benefited from exposure to a constant stream of religious, cultural and political influences from the mainland. Strategically situated across the ocean trade routes around the tip of South Asia, its ports hosted ships not only from South Asia, but also from the Hellenistic West and Southeast Asia and later from Muslim and Chinese traders. Throughout its history, Sri Lanka's unique proximity to the mainland and its position on important international trade routes have contributed to the development of a cosmopolitan civilization. Its position as an island has allowed Sri Lanka to evolve a distinct culture and civilization.

At the heart of the island of Sri Lanka is a mountainous region that feeds rivers that run to the coast. These mountains assist in creating three climatic zones. A dry zone covers the northern half of the island and extends down its eastern coast. The southwest corner of the island receives heavy rain, while the rest of the island has moderate rainfall. Most of the rainfall follows the monsoon between October and January. As a result of the moist, tropical climate, much of the island is covered with thick forests.

From the beginning of its recorded history, Sri Lanka has had a multi-ethnic population. Around 500 B.C., Indo-Aryan people from North India mixed with the local population. Today, they form the Sinhalese ethnic group and comprise approximately 74% of the population. Beginning in the 3rd-century B.C., Dravidian people from South India arrived and eventually came to comprise 18% of the population. Over the centuries, other people arrived, and today the descendents of Arab traders make up 7% of the population. Sinhalese civilization first emerged in the dry zone and soon flourished due to the development of a complex irrigation system that was one of

The Art of Sri Lanka   53

the most sophisticated in the ancient world. By the first century B.C., a network of earthen dams harnessed the rivers and distributed water through a system of irrigation canals. About the same time, a centralized state was developed with its capital at Anuradhapura in the dry zone. For over 1,000 years Anuradhapura was to remain the political and religious center of Sri Lanka.

The history of Sinhalese art is the history of Buddhist religious art, just as the great chronicles of Sinhalese history, the *Mahavamsa* and the *Chulavamsa*, are literally the history of the Buddhist religion in Sri Lanka.[1] According to the *Mahavamsa*, Buddhism was introduced to Sri Lanka by Mahinda, the son of the South Asian emperor Asoka (c. 272–231 B.C.). Arriving in the capital city of Anuradhapura during the reign of king Devanampiyatissa (250–210 B.C.), Mahinda quickly converted the king and his court to Buddhism and was rewarded by the king with a garden that would eventually become the great Mahavihara monastery. Later, through magic powers, Asoka's grandson, Sumana, brought the Buddha's alms bowl and collarbone to be enshrined

in a reliquary mound (*stupa*) at the monastery and Mahinda's sister, Samghamitta, arrived with a cutting of the Bodhi tree under which the Buddha had achieved enlightenment. With the founding and royal patronage of the first Buddhist monasteries in Sri Lanka, a pattern was established in which the role of the king was to support the Buddhist monastic order and, in turn, the Buddhist order gave legitimacy to the king's rule. This system of reciprocal patronage became the model that virtually all kings who followed emulated. Among the primary duties of the king was to build monasteries and commission the making of the Buddha images that were enshrined within them.

Today, there is only one major Buddhist order in Sri Lanka, the orthodox "Lineage of the Elders," Theravada, whose parent monastery is the Mahavihara. This is also the Buddhist order that has traditionally been the most important in Burma, Thailand and post 13th-century Cambodia. Today, the majority of Buddhist monasteries in those countries also hold the Mahavihara as their ultimate source. The Theravadans trace their lineage of teachers back to

Mahinda and the introduction of Buddhism into Sri Lanka. There are some minor divisions in interpretation, which have developed into sub-lineages, but all Theravadans observe the same basic code of monastic behavior, *vinaya*, and textual tradition, *tripitaka*.

The Theravadans are only one of many Buddhist religious orders that took root in Sri Lanka and received royal patronage and wide popular support. Most of what we know about the different orders is recorded in the *Mahavamsa* and *Chulavamsa*. These chronicles were written from the perspective of the monks of the orthodox Mahavihara and are highly critical of competing orders from both the standpoint of doctrinal practice and as recipients of royal gifts. As a result, the historical records concerning the development of Buddhism in Sri Lanka are incomplete and do not include many significant events.

As Buddhist philosophy and practice evolved in South Asia, changes also occurred in how the Buddha and other deities were depicted. These changes were iconographic and stylistic, as well as iconometric. As Sri Lanka was part of a well-connected and cosmopolitan Buddhist world, it was greatly influenced by contemporary South Asian changes in Buddhist religious practice and art. During the 2nd-century B.C., before the first Buddha images were being made at Amaravati and imported into Sri Lanka, the great Mahayana teacher Nagarjuna was active in South Asia. Even if Sinhalese monks strictly followed the orthodox Theravada school of the Mahavihara, in the course of pilgrimages to the monasteries that had grown up around sites associated with the Buddha's life and South Asian monastic universities, they would have been aware of Buddha images made in new styles, some of which they brought with them on their return.

The first major division in Sri Lankan Buddhism came with the founding of the Abhayagiri monastery by King Vattagamani Abhaya (103 B.C., restored to throne 89-77 B.C.) as a gift for a favorite monk. The monks of the Mahavihara attacked those of the new monastery as it challenged their influence and monopoly on royal patronage. Though initially doctrinally the same, the schism created circumstances that would eventually facilitate the adoption of Mahayana Buddhism by the monks of the Abhayagiri. South Asian monks who followed teachings proscribed by the Mahavihara would more likely than not be able to find lodging and places to debate their views at the Abhayagiri. By the reign of Mahasena (274-301), the Abhayagiri was known in South Asia as the center of Sinhalese Mahayana Buddhism.[2] In 846, during the reign of Sena I (833-853), the first Vajrayana Buddhist monk came to Sri Lanka. He was given a place to stay and teach at the Abhayagiri monastery.[3]

As a result of these continuing waves of influence, Sri Lankan Buddhist art displays an immense range of styles and iconometric trends. Some influences were minor and confined to a relatively small group of practitioners and their patrons, and thus left only a few images in that style. Others were widely practiced and received royal patronage over a long period of time; numerous images in those styles have survived.

The late Anuradhapura period is marked by times of peace and prosperity interspersed with civil war and conquest by foreign armies. Successive waves of foreign influence contributed to the rapid development of Sri Lanka's political, economic and religious culture. Traveling throughout India to places of pilgrimage for religious instruction, sanctuary and support, Sri Lankan Buddhist monks were exposed to the latest Buddhist teachings. In return, noted teachers such as Buddhaghosa took up residence in Sri Lankan monasteries and contributed to the island's vital and growing religious climate.

In 432, Anuradhapura was sacked by invading armies from South India, but by 459 Sri Lanka regained its independence under the leadership of Dhatusena (reigned 459-477) and entered into a period of great prosperity and religious patronage. He refurbished or rebuilt numerous monuments in both the Mahavihara and the Abhayagiri monasteries. Between 618 and 684, petty feuds led to civil war and created the opportunity for the Pallava king to invade Sri Lanka. No sooner had Sri Lanka regained its independence than a disenfranchised Sinhalese prince took refuge at the Pallava court and, with its backing, succeeded in taking the Sinhalese throne in 689. This ushered in a period of close relations between the Sinhalese and Pallava kings, which ended with the fall of the Pallavas and the subsequent conquest of Anuradhapura by the Cholas in 993.

In 993 the armies of the Chola king Rajaraja I (983-1014) defeated the Sinhalese and sacked Anuradhapura, while the Sinhalese king Mahinda V (982-1029) fled to the southern province of Rohuna. The Cholas made the city of Polonnaruva their capital and ruled the entire northern portion of Sri Lanka, including Anuradhapura, from there. In 1070 the armies of Vijayabahu I (1055-1110) drove the Cholas from Polonnaruva and he made it his capital.

During the Chola occupation, state support of the great Buddhist monasteries of Anuradhapura ended, as the Cholas were Hindus who founded and patronized numerous Hindu shrines. While the Cholas were Hindus, they did not persecute Buddhists, and there is evidence that they occasionally patronized small local Buddhist monasteries. In the south, organizing armed resistance to the invaders took all of the resources of the Sinhalese king and nobles.

Without strong royal patronage, the Buddhist order declined drastically. According to the *Chulavamsa*, by the time Polonnaruva was liberated, there were not enough Buddhist monks remaining in Sri Lanka to hold a valid ordination ceremony. Because of this, Vijayabahu sent a mission to King Annuruddha of Burma (1044-1077) requesting that the required number of monks needed to conduct ordinations and re-establish the Buddhist order be sent to Sri Lanka.[4]

After the death of Vijayabahu, the Sinhalese once again fell to quarrelling among themselves and the country was divided into three rival kingdoms. King Parakramabahu I (1153-1186) succeeded in once again unifying the country and claimed Polonnaruva as his capital. The reign of Parakramabahu and that of his successor Nissamkamalla (1187-1196) was a period of peace and prosperity during which the Buddhist institutions flourished and there was a renaissance of Sinhalese art and architecture. This renaissance saw a new wave of South Indian influence not only in architecture, but also in sculpture.

Bringing their own craftsmen from South India, the Cholas had constructed numerous Hindu shrines in stone and brick, and had cast many fine statues of Hindu deities in bronze. When the Sinhalese conquered Polonnaruva, they in turn employed many South Indian architects, artists and artisans in the making of Buddhist monasteries and sculptures. Buddhist sculpture closely followed mainland styles, with the sculptural style of the flourishing monastic community of Nagapattinam near Travancore in South India exerting a strong influence.

Throughout the later part of the Polonnaruva period and into the early 13th century, generals rebelled against the Sinhalese kings and infighting weakened the country, making it an attractive target for successive waves of invasions from South India. The last king of Polonnaruva, Parakrama Pandya (1212-1215), was a Pandyan prince from South India. In 1232 the armies of the Kalinga prince Magha (1215-1236) invaded Sri Lanka and captured the entire northern part of the country, including Polonnaruva, and imprisoned the Pandyan king. With the loss

of Polonnaruva, various kingdoms competed with one another for political pre-eminence, first at the rock fortress of Dambadenya, and later at such sites as Yapahuva and Gampola. This period has been termed by Sinhalese historians as the Period of Divided Kingdoms. Against the background of these internecine conflicts, successive waves of European imperialists arrived, first the Portuguese and later the Dutch. These colonial powers eventually conquered and controlled parts of the island. The Portuguese, especially, destroyed both Buddhist and Hindu temples. The troubles of the Buddhist order during the Period of Divided Kingdoms reached a peak during the reign of King Rajasinha I (1582-1591), when a number of Buddhist monks were implicated in conspiring with the Portuguese to depose him. According to the *Chulavamsa*:

He annihilated the order of the Victor, slew the community of the bhikkhus, *burned the sacred books, destroyed the monasteries and thus barred his way to heaven...At that time through fear of the King,* bhikkhus *left the Order...*[5]

Kandy emerged as the capital of one of several competing Sinhalese kingdoms when Sensammata Vikramabahu (1469-1511) established his court there. Located high in a series of easily defensible mountain valleys, the Kingdom of Kandy alone withstood the pressures of the European invaders. As the Europeans expanded their influence throughout the lowland kingdoms, the king of Kandy became the sole champion of Buddhism throughout the island. After Rajasinha I's persecution of the Buddhist order, there was little support for the order and the number of monks declined to the point at which, during the reign of the Kandyan king Vimaladharmasurya I (1591-1604), it is recorded in the *Chulavamsa* that:

"*As there were no* bhikkhus *in the island of Lanka on whom the ceremony of admission to the Order had been performed, the King sent officials to the country of Rakkhanga (the Burmese province of Arakan), invited Nandicakka and other* bhikkhus*, and made them take up their abode in the noble city of Sirivaddhana (Kandy) and cared for them*

in reverent manner…thither in the year two thousand one hundred and forty after the nirvana of the Victor (1596), he led the bhikkhus*, had the ceremony of admission to the Order performed on many of the sons of good family and thus protected the Order of the Enlightened One.*"[6]

Vimaladharmasurya I also brought the Tooth Relic, the palladium of the Kingdom of Sri Lanka, to Kandy, marking the city's emergence as the capital of the island. During the reign of his son, Senarat (1604-1635), the Portuguese actively expanded their influence throughout the coastal areas:

"*They spread themselves over several fair provinces, laid waste fields and gardens, burned down houses and villages, destroyed the noble families and in this wise brought ruin on Sihala. They broke into the towns, into the relic shrines and monasteries, destroyed the image houses, Bodhi trees, Buddha statues, and so on, did great harm to the laity and the Order…*"[7]

In despair, Rajasinha II (1635-1687) formed an alliance with the Dutch, who succeeded in driving the Portuguese from

Kirti Sri Rajasinha
Period: 18th Century
Cave #3—Dambulla
IMAGE 1

the lowlands. However, during the reign of Vimaladharmasurya II (1687-1707) the status of the Buddhist order had fallen so low that the king once again brought a group of Buddhist monks from Arakan to hold valid ordinations and strengthen the Sinhalese Buddhist order.

The last Sinhalese king of Kandy died in 1747 without either a son or daughter who could succeed him to the throne. As there were no suitable Sinhalese candidates and his chief queen was a princess of the Nayak dynasty of Madurai, both his ministers and the head of the Buddhist order agreed to invite one of her brothers to ascend the throne. Thus a Nayakkar Hindu prince who was a follower of Siva became the king of Kandy as Sri Vijaya Rajasinha (1739-1747). Upon assuming the throne, he converted to Theravada Buddhism and became an enthusiastic patron of it. Despite extreme pressures

from Sinhalese nobility and factions within the Buddhist order, the first kings of the Nayakkar dynasty at Kandy were able to consolidate their positions and rule successfully due to their ability to adopt the role of the traditional Buddhist monarch that had been established by King Devanampiyatissa (250–210 B.C.). Sri Vijaya Rajasinha's son, Kirti Sri Rajasinha (1747-1782), is still revered by the Sinhalese as one of the most fervent patrons of Buddhism (IMAGE 1). He invigorated the Sinhalese Buddhist order by bringing monks from the Thai kingdom of Ayutthaya to hold new ordinations, refurbished many monastic establishments that had fallen into disrepair and founded numerous others. Today it is hard to visit a temple dating from or prior to his reign that has not benefited from his patronage. Most of the Buddha images produced during the Kandyan period were created during his rule.

END NOTES

1 These two texts are literally titled the "Greater and Lesser Chronicles," *Mahavamsa* and *Chulavamsa*. *Mahavamsa*, trans. W. Geiger (Colombo, 1950). *Chulavamsa*, trans. W. Geiger, 2 vols., (Colombo: Ceylon Government Information Department, 1953).

2 Walpola Rahula, *History of Buddhism in Ceylon*, (Colombo: M. D. Gunasena & Co., Ltd., 1966) 96-97. Diran Dohanian feels that the monks of the Abhayagiri had adopted only a few Mahayana concepts, such as worship of Bodhisattvas and the belief that Buddha was the ultimate destiny of all sentient beings, at a later date. He presents that their practice was essentially the same as that followed by the monks of the Mahavihara. See Diran Dohanian, *The Mahayana Buddhist Sculpture of Ceylon*, (New York: Garland Publishing Inc., 1977) 8-11.

3 The name of this monk is unknown, but it is recorded that the monks of the Abhayagiri gave him initial support. Rahula, 109.

4 This currently varies among the different Theravada lineages.

5 *Chulavamsa*, 224-226.

6 *Chulavamsa*, 228-229.

7 *Chulavamsa*, 231-232.

ANURADHAPURA PERIOD

269 B.C.–993 A.D.

Standing Buddha at Avukana—Sri Lanka

Buddha Images
OF THE EARLY ANURADHAPURA PERIOD

(c. 200 B.C. — 432 A.D.)

John Listopad—Stanford University

Despite references to royally commissioned Buddha images in the great chronicle of Sinhalese history, the *Mahavamsa*, no Sri Lankan Buddha images have been discovered that can be dated prior to the 3rd-century A.D. All of the early Buddha images found follow closely the style of the great Buddhist monastic center of Amaravati in the Krishna River valley of Southwest India. In this style both the head and cranial protuberance, *usnisa*, are covered with short curls of hair tightly twisted into spirals. The *usnisa* is very low, the face is blocky, and the eyes are wide open and stare straight ahead. Unlike images from Amaravati, Sri Lankan images in the Amaravati style do not have the characteristic round tuft of hair on the forehead, the *urna*. Standing images are almost always made in stone; very few standing images made of bronze have been found. When the images are seated, they are always depicted in the posture known as *virasana* with the right leg placed on top of the left leg with only the sole of the right foot visible. Bodies are relatively heavy and

massive in form, being broadly and simply fashioned, and the width of the hips and shoulders are roughly the same. It is the treatment of the robe, however, that is perhaps the most important defining characteristic of this and later Sinhalese sculptural styles. In these early images, the robe is thick; the forms of the body are barely revealed through it. The fabric is pleated and the folds run diagonally across the body in a subtle and varied rhythm of incised lines that serve to animate the surface of the sculpture. In standing images the over-garment, *uttarasanga*, is draped over the left shoulder, leaving the right shoulder bare. It is very long and is lifted up by the left forearm, which is raised towards the left shoulder. On the outside of the arm, it falls directly down in a straight line; to the right, it hangs down to form a broad swag just above the lower hem of the undergarment, *antaravasaka*. The hem of the *uttarasanga* hangs straight down the back from the shoulder. Almost without exception, the right hand is raised in the gesture of

Head of Buddha
Anuradhapura Period: 5th–6th Century
Dolomite
H 34.3cm W 24.2cm D 24cm
IMAGE 1

reassurance, *abhaya mudra*, and the left hand is raised, clenched with its back facing the viewer. It generally does not appear to actually be grasping the *uttarasanga*.

The *Head of Buddha* (IMAGE 1) displays several early characteristics, though it very likely is slightly later in date. The *usnisa* is very low, and both it and the head are covered with tightly wound curls of hair. The eyes are wide open and stare straight ahead. Originally they would have been inlaid with painted crystal or stone, a feature not usually encountered in Buddha images from Amaravati. The rather narrow proportion of the face and small mouth are characteristics that relate it to the 5th to 6th-century of the later phase of sculpture at Anuradhapura.

Buddha Images
OF THE LATE ANURADHAPURA PERIOD (C. 432 — 993)

John Listopad—Stanford University

As in the preceding period, the Buddhist art of Amaravati exerted a tremendous influence on the development of Sinhalese art. However, the art of Amaravati was undergoing stylistic changes due to the influence of the art of the great monastic universities and pilgrimage sites in Bihar and Bengal, as well as the distinctive art of the Eastern Chalukyas. Close contacts with the Hindu Pallava court also were reflected in exchanges between Sinhalese and South Indian monastic institutions.[1] By the fall of Anuradhapura in 993, virtually all the schools of religious thought that were active in Northern and Southern South Asia were either being practiced or were known about in Sri Lanka. The result is that the art of the later Anuradhapura period, while still paying homage to the early aesthetic and iconographic style of Amaravati, gradually begins to diversify.

One of the key images in the development of Sinhalese Buddhist art is the monumental standing Buddha image at Avukana (IMAGE 2). This monumental image

Buddha
Anuradhapura Period: 8th Century
Avukana—Sri Lanka
IMAGE 2

has been convincingly attributed to the 8th century and displays many characteristics that highlight the changes in sculpture between the early and late Anuradhapura periods.[2] It differs from the earlier Amaravati-inspired images in that the shoulders are broader than the waist and the forms of the body are full and fleshy, clearly distinguished beneath the robe, as is the string belt that holds up the lower garment. The

Head of Buddha
Anuradhapura Period: 6th Century
Dolomite
H 40cm W 27cm D 29cm
IMAGE 3

details of the face have much sharper edges and the eyes are half closed, as if in contemplation.

The *Head of Buddha* (IMAGE 3) demonstrates subtle changes from the early Anuradhapura style. The *usnisa* is larger and more prominent and the eyes are no longer wide open and staring ahead, but are half-closed, suggesting a date in the 6th century. Like IMAGE 1, the eyes would have been inlaid with painted crystal or stone. The hairline is relatively straight across the forehead. A heavily weathered *Enthroned Buddha* displays other characteristics that are different from images of the early Anuradhapura period, even though its eyes are wide open and stare straight ahead (IMAGE 4). Seated against a throne whose crossbars end in the heads of two mythical aquatic creatures, *makara*, the Buddha sits with his right leg placed on his left in the *virasana* posture. His hands rest palm up, one on top of one another, in the attitude of meditation, *samadhi* or *dhyana mudra*. The shoulders are emphatically wider than the hips and the waist is pinched. The arms are tapered. There is no evidence of pleats in either the upper or lower robe. The line of the belt holding up the *antaravasaka* is clearly defined; there is an awareness and appreciation of the surface of the body. The *usnisa* is smaller and more conical than that of IMAGE 3, suggesting movement back towards the smaller *usnisa* of the early Anuradhapura style. All of these stylistic innovations are characteristic of Gupta and post-Gupta sculpture, indicating a new source of stylistic influence and possibly the presence of the Mahayana sect of Buddhism.

Because of these characteristics, it most likely dates from the 5th or 6th-century. Images with wide-open eyes, usually standing Buddhas and Bodhisattvas, continued to be made through the late Anuradhapura period. The downwards-looking, half-closed introspective gaze of most seated late Anuradhapura period Buddha images was recognized as more appropriate to the practice of meditation and not other activities.

A bronze sculpture of a Buddha seated in *virasana* with his right hand raised in the gesture of discourse with the thumb touching the forefinger, *vitarka mudra*, and his left hand almost closed in the "gesture of inviting and giving" *ahuyavarada mudra*,[6] also has the same treatment of the body (IMAGE 5). It displays the same broad shoulders, pinched waist, and thin, smooth robes worn with the right shoulder bare as the stone IMAGE 4. There are, however, important differences in the way that the mass of the body is conceived. Buddha images with thin, smooth robes and the right shoulder bare were most popular in the western Deccan, and most likely entered the stylistic

vocabulary of the Buddhist art of Amaravati and the rest of South India at some point in the 6th or 7th-century.[4] The waist is fleshier than that of the stone IMAGE 4, the hands and feet are more firmly modeled, the hem of the edge of the robe across his chest is raised, and the robe falls in gently undulating folds from both sides of his left arm to his thighs. The *usnisa* is low and broad

Enthroned Buddha
Anuradhapura Period: 5th–6th Century
Dolomite
H 51cm W 41cm D 17cm
IMAGE 4

Seated Preaching Buddha
Anuradhapura Period: 6th–7th Century
Bronze, Hollow-cast
H 13.4cm W 10.2cm D 4.5cm
IMAGE 5

as in the early Anuradhapura head, but the eyes are half-closed. This combination of gestures, along with the modeling of the hands, feet and robe, and the lack of a flame, *sirispata*, on top of the *usnisa* suggest a date in the 6th to 7th-century.

From the 8th-century onwards, most bronze Sri Lankan Buddha images were made with a flame, *sirispata*, on top of the *usnisa* (IMAGE 6). As time progressed, these *sirispata* became elaborate and were often inlaid with jewels. The hairline across the forehead changed from being straight across to having a pronounced dip in the center.[5] At some point during the 8th-century, two more stylistic innovations also became common in Sri Lankan seated Buddha images: the shawl, *sanghati*, was depicted folded neatly and draped over the shoulder, and the folded hem of the robe hangs down from the shoulder across the arm to the thighs, as can be seen in this 9th-century image (IMAGE 7). A *sanghati* does not appear on standing images until the Divided Kingdoms Period. While the *sirispata* is very likely a Sinhalese stylistic innovation, the depiction of the *sanghati* or

Seated Buddha
Anuradhapura Period: 8th Century
Bronze, Hollow-cast
H 12.7cm W 10.5cm D 4cm
IMAGE 6

Seated Buddha
Anuradhapura Period: 9th Century
Bronze
H 18cm W 15.5cm D 8cm
IMAGE 7

Seated Buddha on Lotus Pedastal
Anuradhapura Period: 9th–10th Century
Bronze
H 7.5cm W 5.6cm D 2.7cm
IMAGE 8

a lappet over the left shoulder is derived from the evolving art of Amaravati, which was in turn responding to the new artistic styles that were becoming popular in the monasteries of Bihar and Bengal. Though it has suffered much from centuries of burial, this Buddha (IMAGE 8) exemplifies the evolving mix of styles during the 9th and 10th centuries. The double lotus base and *sanghati* over the left shoulder suggest the influence of Bihar and Bengal; the *sirispata* is a relatively recent iconographic innovation, and the pleated robe is a reference to the Buddha images of the early Amaravati and Anuradhapura styles.[6]

Only two images in this exhibition can be associated with Buddha images that come from a known excavation. IMAGE 9 is virtually identical to a group of over 50 Buddha images that were found in a hoard totalling more than 100 at the Veragal Sirisangabo Vihara at Allavava in Anuradhapura district, and with a group of 14 images found at the Toluvila Vihara at Anuradhapura. All of these are generally accepted as dating from the 10th-century. Many are virtually identical and were very likely cast from wax

Seated Buddha
Anuradhapura Period: 10th Century
Gilt Bronze
H 11.7cm W 8.5cm D 4.5cm
IMAGE 9

Seated Buddha
Anuradhapura Period: 10th Century
Gilt Bronze
H 10.7cm W 9.5cm D 3.9cm
IMAGE 10

cores mass-produced from a single clay mold. All of these images were modeled, the curls of the hair were simply stamped, the *sanghati* was indicated by shallow incised lines, and only minimal attention was paid to finishing details. This reflects the tendency of many late Anuradhapura Buddha images to reflect contemporary Buddhist art under the Pallavas, where the elements of the torso, face, hands, feet and robe were simply and summarily treated. IMAGE 10 is very similar to IMAGE 9, except that it was much more finely modeled prior to casting and great care was paid to finishing it. It is possible that the wax core on which it was based was made from a mold similar to that used for IMAGE 9 and the figures from the Veragal Sirisangabo and Toluvila Viharas.

In addition to these external changes, Sinhalese artists began to cast images of solid metal during the late Anuradhapura period. This was most likely due to the growing influence of the South Indian Hindu proscriptions about making hollow images as outlined in the slightly later text, the *Sariputra* (see *The Cult of the Buddha Image*, page 41).

Head of Buddha
Anuradhapura Period: 5th–6th Century
Dolomite
H 34.3cm W 24.2cm D 24cm

Head of Buddha
Anuradhapura Period
6th Century
Dolomite
H 40cm W 27cm D 29cm

Head of Buddha
Anuradhapura Period: 6th Century
Dolomite
H 40cm   W 28cm   D 32cm

Enthroned Buddha
Anuradhapura Period: 5th–6th Century
Dolomite
H 51cm W 41cm D 17cm

Seated Buddha Preaching
Anuradhapura Period
6th Century
Bronze, Hollow-cast
H 13.4cm W 10.2cm D 4.5cm

Seated Buddha
Anuradhapura Period
8th Century
Bronze, Hollow-cast
H 12.7cm W 10.5cm D 4cm

Seated Buddha
Anuradhapura Period: 9th Century
Bronze
H 18cm W 15.5cm D 8cm

Seated Buddha
Anuradhapura Period: 9th–10th Century
Bronze
H 12.5cm w 11.5cm D 6cm

Seated Buddha on Lotus Pedestal
Anuradhapura Period: 9th–10th Century
Bronze
H 7.5cm w 5.6cm D 2.7cm

Seated Buddha
Anuradhapura Period: 10th Century
Gilt Bronze
H 11.2cm w 8.5cm D 4.5cm

Seated Buddha
Anuradhapura Period: 10th Century
Bronze with Traces of Gilt
H 8 w 7.2cm D 3.4cm

Seated Buddha
Anuradhapura Period
9th–10th Century
Gilt Bronze
H 10.7cm W 9.5cm D 3.9cm

Seated Buddha
Anuradhapura Period: 9th–10th Century
Bronze
H 13.3cm W 10.4cm D 5cm

Jambhala
Anuradhapura Period: 9th–10th Century
Bronze
H 9.5cm W 7cm D 6cm

Architects Plummet or Palanquin Hook
Anuradhapura Period or Early Polonnaruva Period: 10th–12th Century
Bronze
H 23cm W 26.5cm D 2.5cm

A Set of Lokapalas
Anuradhapura Period: 9th Century
Bronze
LEFT TO RIGHT: Indra, Yama, Brahma, Varuna and Kubera

A Set of Lokapalas

ANURADHAPURA PERIOD

John Listopad—Stanford University

This group of five deities represents Brahma, Lord of the Center or Zenith; and the regents of the four directions or *lokapalas*: Indra, the Regent of the East; Yama, the Regent of the South; Varuna, the Regent of the West; and Kubera, the Regent of the North. Their iconography, iconometry and ritual placement in conjunction with the foundation of a monastery are carefully described in Mahayana Buddhist iconographic and ritual texts such as the *Vastuvidya Sastra*.[1] While they are Brahmanic deities properly belonging to the Hindu religion, in some sects of Mahayana Buddhism they were adopted as protectors of the Buddhist religion. The *lokapalas* are always depicted with royal attributes. They are the rulers of the spheres and the kings of the three worlds of existence of traditional Buddhist cosmology. All Buddhist and Hindu sacred architecture is based on upon the conceptual division of the spheres of these deities. They are invoked at the building of a temple or the planning of a city and during certain rituals.

Brahma is mentioned in the Tantras as the "Immense Being" and the "Giver of Knowledge" whose realm is the zenith. It is appropriate that he is placed at the center of a new monastery in his form as Visvakarman, the architect of the universe. He is depicted with 4 faces and 8 arms standing on a tortoise. His front and rear pairs of arms are raised in *anjali mudra*. His upper right hand holds what may have been a ladle for ritual sacrifice, *sruk*, and his lower right arm holds a ritual staff, *danda*. His upper left hand holds a conch shell, *shanka*, and while his lower left hand is broken off, it may have held one of a number of attributes.

Indra, the regent of the East, is the lord of the gods and protector of heroes and represents the power of the thunderbolt. Here he is depicted with two arms raised in *anjali mudra*, one hand holds the thunderbolt, *vajra*, and the other is held over his mount the elephant.

Varuna, "*the Coverer or Binder*," the regent of the West is the lord of Knowledge.

He rules over the invisible world and his power is said to be felt during the night and in all that is mysterious, beyond the understanding of man. He is considered to be the lord of the waters, both of the sea and subterranean, and his domain is the Western Ocean. His vehicle as a *lokapala* is a horse. In this example he is depicted with two hands raised in *anjali mudra*, his left hand that is now broken would have held a noose, his right hovers over his mount.

Kubera, the regent of the north, is the lord of wealth. He rules over the spirits who guard the precious stones and wealth within the earth. As a *lokapala* he is depicted with two hands raised in *anjali mudra*, a mace held in his right hand and his left raised over his mount, the lion.

Yama, "the Binder," the regent of the South, is the lord of Death. Various texts hold that the virtuous and the evil see Yama in different forms. To those who have done wrong he appears as fearful and grim, with dark green complexion and glowing red eyes. To the virtuous his face is charming and smiling, his eyes are like open lotuses, and he wears a crown, earrings and a garland of flowers. He is described as riding or being accompanied by the a buffalo. He most often holds a staff and a noose. Here Yama is depicted as greeting the virtuous, with two of his hands raised in the gesture of respect and salutation, *anjali mudra*. His other two hands hold the staff of death (only the handle remains) and gestures protectively over his buffalo mount.

According to the *Vastuvidyasastra*, before a monastery was built, the architect would lay out a grid over the proposed plan, establishing series of squares, each of which would be dedicated to a particular deity.[2] After the squares had been laid out and each assigned a specific deity, the ritual of the symbolic impregnation of the site, *garbha-vidhana*, was observed. During this ritual an object representing the appropriate deity was placed in each of the 25 squares that were specifically dedicated to the deities of the site. In the squares of the 4 deities who were the regents of the 4 directions; Indra, Yama, Varuna and Kubera; a statue of each respective deity would be placed instead of a symbolic object. *"[A figure] of Indra should be placed*

Brahma on a Turtle
Anuradhapura Period: 10th Century
Bronze
H 33cm W 15cm D 14cm
IMAGE 1

in the Suryamsa [to the East]...In the Yamamsa [to the South] there should be [a figure of] Yamadeva...In the Varunamsa [to the West] there shall be a figure of Varunna...In the Soma [to the North] there shall be a figure of Kubera in the center [Brahmamsa] the figure of Brahma seated on the lotus-seat, with his eyes casting the even glance...On its left should be a figure of a tortoise ..." [3] All of the images would be placed facing inwards, except that of Brahma, who would be positioned so that his principal face was oriented to the East. These are among the finest images of Brahma and the four lokapalas that have come to the attention of the scholarly community. Buried in a stone or brick chamber, most images of this type were subjected to a high degree of moisture and salts leached from within the soil. As they were created to be in the foundation deposit of a religious edifice, they are usually relatively small in scale, simply formed with less surface detail and less finely finished than images made for worship. Though the artist must have been familiar with the aesthetic tradition that produced the 9th- or 10th-century set of four *lokapalas* found under the four porches of the Pubbarama Vihara of the Puliyankulam in Anuradhapura, the diamond-shaped lozenges on the crown of Brahma are not found in the art of contemporary Sri Lankan and South Indian images, but they are commonly found on contemporary sculptures from the region that is now Bangladesh. [4] Also the handling of the waist and torso seem also to have been influenced by the Buddhist sculpture of northeastern South Asia. A date in the 10th-century, during the late Anuradhapura period, is suggested by the remedial bows on the hips of the images and the folds of cloth on the legs which are derived from Pallava sculpture. On Pallava images of the eighth and ninth centuries they are generally much more pronounced, on Chola images made in Sri Lanka they are lacking.

Images such as this set of *lokapalas* provide a glimpse into the complex religious atmosphere and cosmopolitan society of the late Anuradhapura period. While the Mahavamsa and Chulavamsa are silent about the practices and makeup of Buddhist

Indra—Regent of the East with Elephant
Anuradhapura Period: 10th Century
Bronze
H 23.5cm   W 13cm   D 10cm
IMAGE 2a

Indra—Regent of the East with Elephant
Anuradhapura Period: 10th Century
Bronze
H 23.5cm   W 13cm   D 10cm
IMAGE 2b

Varuna—Regent of the West with Horse
Anuradhapura Period: 10th Century
Bronze
H 23.5cm   W 9.8cm   D 12cm
IMAGE 3a

Varuna—Regent of the West with Horse
Anuradhapura Period: 10th Century
Bronze
H 23.5cm   W 9.8cm   D 12cm
IMAGE 3b

Kubera—Regent of the North with Lion
Anuradhapura Period: 10th Century
Bronze
H 23.5cm W 14cm D 19.5cm
IMAGE 4a

Kubera—Regent of the North with Lion
Anuradhapura Period: 10th Century
Bronze
H 23.5cm W 14cm D 19.5cm
IMAGE 4b

Yama—Regent of the South with Buffalo
Anuradhapura Period: 10th Century
Bronze
H 23.5cm W 9cm D 10cm
IMAGE 5a

Yama—Regent of the South with Buffalo
Anuradhapura Period: 10th Century
Bronze
H 23.5cm W 9cm D 10cm
IMAGE 5b

sects with whom they disagreed, it is clear that not only were tantric texts being studied by Sri Lankan Buddhist monks, but that they were also very likely informed by visits of religious teachers from northeastern India, who also brought religious images in a different style with them. Religious and artistic influences from diverse areas of South Asia came together and blended together at Anuradhapura to create new artistic styles, a process that continued throughout the Polonnaruva, Divided Kingdoms, and Kandyan periods.

END NOTES

1 The *Vastuvidya Sastra* ascribed to Manjusri, E. W. Marasinghe trans., (Delhi, Sri Satguru Publications, 1989). The *Vastuvidaya Sastra* is a Sanskrit language text that provided a guide to building a monastery and constructing or repairing the images within one. We do not know which Mahayana sect it was associated with, or which monasteries were built using it as a guide. It was most likely written in Sri Lanka during the late Anuradhapura period.

2 The *Vastuvidya Sastra* discusses which of the 24 types of monasteries would be suitable for any given site. Depending upon the type of monastery, a grid would be laid out establishing squares dedicated to specific guardian deities. Depending on the type of monastery these plans could contain 9, 25, 45, 64 or 81 squares with their accompanying deity. There are some iconographic differences between the images of the *lokapalas* and Brahma as described in the *Vastuvidya Sastra* and this set. At present we do not know exactly which text supplied the iconographic information for this group of *lokapalas,* but based on stylistic influences from northeastern South Asia (see below), it was very likely a northern Mahayana or Vajrayana text.

3 *Vastuvidya Sastra,* 41-43. In contrast to the image of Brahma standing on a tortoise in this exhibition, the *Vastuvidya Sastra* specifies that the images of Brahma and the tortoise were to be made separately.

4 The Pubbarama *lokapalas* are published in von Schoeder, *Buddhist Sculpture of Sri Lanka,* 300-301.

POLONNARUVA PERIOD

993–1235

Monumental Reclining Buddha—Gal Vihara

Polonnaruva Period (993—1235)

John Listopad—Stanford University

To commemorate a council reconciling the different Buddhist orders, Parakramabahu I created three of the Buddha images at the Gal Vihara in Polonnaruva. A large seated Buddha in an artificial cave displays many characteristics of Chola Buddhist sculpture (IMAGE 1). The face is rounder than those of the late Anuradhapura period. The folds of the robes are more stylized and reduced to a pattern of incised parallel lines, a technique seen in a slightly different manner in both Pallava and Chola stone sculpture. The hairline is similar to that of Chola Buddha images, except that it is higher on the forehead. Proportionally, the hair covers less of the head than the Buddha images of the early Anuradhapura period. The *sanghati* is elaborately folded and placed over the left shoulder with a hem of cloth continuing from its lower corner across the arm and down over the left thigh. There is a calm serenity to the image, an abstraction or simplification reflecting contemporary South Asian trends already apparent in late Anuradhapura images.

Buddha (IMAGE 2) displays many characteristics of Buddhist sculpture at Nagapattinam. Like many late Anuradhapura images that were also inspired by South Indian sculptural styles, the body and garments are executed with minimal detail. The head is much more round when compared with the faces of late Anuradhapura period Buddha images, similar to that in the cave at the Gal Vihara.

Seated Buddha
Polonnaruva Period: 12th–13th Century
Gal Vihara—Sri Lanka
IMAGE 1

Seated Buddha under Makara Torana
Polonnaruva Period: 12th–13th Century
Bronze with Traces of Gilt
H 27cm W 9cm D 3.5cm
IMAGE 2

Parallel double lines indicate the hems of the robes. The treatment of the hair like an inverted cup with a sharp line separating it from the forehead is characteristic of South Indian Buddha images made under the Cholas. The Buddha is seated on a throne backed by a simplified *makara torana*, in the manner of contemporary South Indian Buddha images. The style of this throne, when compared to South Indian examples, assists in dating this image to the 12th–13th century. IMAGE 3 also displays the characteristic Chola treatment of the hair, but the face has become more oval and the details of the robe have become more pronounced, indicating a slightly later date in the 13th–14th century.

Seated Buddha
Polonnaruva Period: 13th–14th Century
Bronze
H 9cm W 6.5cm
IMAGE 3

Shiva Nataraja
Polonnaruva Period
12th Century
Bronze
H 28cm W 24cm D 8.6cm

Shiva Nataraja
(Side view)

Seated Buddha
Polonnaruva Period: 12th–13th Century
Bronze
H 11cm w 8cm

Seated Buddha
Polonnaruva Period: 12th–13th Century
Bronze
H 9cm w 6.5cm

Seated Buddha
Polonnaruva Period: 12th–13th Century
Bronze
H 11cm w 11cm

Seated Buddha
Polonnaruva Period: 12th–13th Century
Bronze
H 9.8cm w 6.5cm

Seated Buddha
Polonnaruva Period
12th–13th Century
Dolomite
H 27cm W 22cm D 7cm

*Seated Buddha
under Makara Torana*
Polonnaruva Period
12th–13th Century
Bronze with Traces of Gilt
H 27cm W 9cm D 3.5cm

Seated Buddha under Makara Torana
Polonnaruva Period: 12th–13th Century
Bronze
H 9.2cm W 5.6cm D 2.6cm

Seated Buddha under Makara Torana
Polonnaruva Period: 12th–13th Century
Bronze
H 12cm W 7cm D 3.6cm

Seated Buddha
Polonnaruva Period: 12th–13th Century
Bronze
H 8.1cm W 5.5cm D 3.9cm

Seated Buddha
Polonnaruva Period: 12th–13th Century
Bronze
H 8.7cm W 6.7cm D 3.4cm

Seated Buddha under Makara Torana
Polonnaruva Period: 12th–13th Century
Bronze
H 8.3cm W 6cm D 4.6cm

Seated Buddha under Makara Torana
Polonnaruva Period: 12th–13th Century
Bronze
H 8cm W 6.2cm D 2.6cm

DIVIDED
KINGDOMS
PERIOD

1232–1597

Seated Buddha—Gadaladeniya Vihara

Divided Kingdoms Period (1232—1597)

John Listopad—Stanford University

For over three hundred years there was no strong central authority and no continuity in patronage of the arts in Sri Lanka. As a result, characteristic of the art of the Period of Divided Kingdoms is the lack of a single style and the amount of variation. A seated Buddha image most likely made during the 15th century displays a number of stylistic elements that are common throughout the Period of Divided Kingdoms: a smooth, thin robe without pleats, an interest in stylizing and experimenting with the hem of the robe and folds of the *sanghati* over the left shoulder, a tuft of hair, *urna*, in the center of the forehead, and a pronounced right nipple (IMAGE 1). Prior to the Divided Kingdoms period, Sri Lankan sculptors generally did not depict the *urna* on their images, despite its almost universal popularity throughout mainland South Asia. Influences that continue from the late Anuradhapura period are the smooth, thin robes and simple schematic bodies. The continuing influence of the Polonnaruva period aesthetic can be seen in faces that tend to be shorter and rounder, with a straight hairline high on the forehead that might have the slightest suggestion of a dip in the center, as in this image. The tops of the ears often rise high alongside the head with their profile more pronounced. While this feature is found occasionally during the late Anuradhapura period and becomes somewhat more common on bronze Polonnaruva period images, it is very common on figures made during the Period of Divided Kingdoms. The subtle smile conveying a sense of omniscience is found on many images from this time and belies the breaks in religious patronage. One other unusual iconographic trait is a smooth neck, lacking any indication of the three folds of flesh depicted on the necks of Buddha images.[7] It is in the treatment of the hems of the robes and the fold of the *sanghati* that the sculptors of the Period of Divided Kingdoms exercised the most creativity and individuality. In this image, the hem of the robe under the right arm is depicted folded down, while under the left

Seated Buddha
Divided Kingdoms Period: 15th Century
Bronze
H 19.5cm W 16cm D 10cm
IMAGE 1

arm the over-garment, *uttarasanga*, has been depicted hanging in three rhythmic folds. This is a simplified version of the treatment of the *uttarasanga* under the left arm on some Polonnaruva period images. The hem with a large fold under the right arm is found on several Buddha images from this period, most notably a bronze standing Buddha in the Morapaya Rajamahavihara in Idampitiya, Nuvara Eliya district, that is dated to the 15th or 16th century.[13]

Many of the same characteristics are found in a less-accomplished Buddha image seated under a *makara torana* topped with a *kirtimukha* (IMAGE 2). Though cast in solid silver, it is aesthetically not as refined as those cast in copper alloys. Images made in precious metals are often less refined, perhaps due to a different group of artisans being responsible for creating and finishing the wax model for the image. The *torana* arch is more stylized than both contemporary stucco examples and examples from the Polonnaruva period. The *stupa* crowning the *kirtimukha* differentiates this example from its Hindu counterparts

Seated Buddha under Makara Torana
Divided Kingdoms Period: 16th Century
Silver
H 20cm W 14cm D 5.8cm
IMAGE 2

and suggests a potential identification of this Buddha with the Buddha of the Future, Maitreya, even though he is not depicted wearing the jewels and crown of a bodhisattva. The artist has enhanced the hem of the robe under the right arm, as in IMAGE 1. He has also delighted in playing with the end of the *sanghati* and the folds of the hem of the *uttarasanga* on the rear of the image. It can be attributed to the 16th century.

Seated Buddha
Divided Kingdoms Period: 16th Century
Bronze
H 8.2cm   W 6cm
IMAGE 3

Standing Buddha
Divided Kingdoms Period: 16th–17th Century
Bronze
H 12.5cm   W 4cm
IMAGE 4

A standing image making the gesture of "fear not" or "reassurance," *abhaya mudra*, with his right hand and the gesture of "giving" or "bestowing," *varada mudra*, with his left hand, demonstrates the same aesthetic characteristics that are present in seated images from the Period of Divided Kingdoms (IMAGE 4). It has a smooth, thin robe without pleats, prominent ears, a large right nipple, pronounced hem under the right arm, and elaborate flourishes at the end of the *sanghati*, both in front and back. While retaining the Polonnaruva treatment of the hairline over the forehead, the head is more oval and elongated in images from the Anuradhapura period and there is no *urna*. The neatly folded *sanghati* over the left shoulder is an innovation in standing images and becomes a standard iconographic feature during this and the following Kandyan period. The folds of the upper garment hang in two symmetrical swags with a slight flourish to the right side, as opposed to the single swag present on standing Buddha images from the Anuradhapura and Polonnaruva periods. This form is most likely derived from the influence of symmetrically splayed robes of Burmese standing Buddha images, a number of which were imported into Sri Lanka through religious missions. This image most likely dates from either the 16th or 17th century.

Another image from the 16th century also displays many of the same characteristics as IMAGE 1: an *urna*, rounded face with sharp features and an almost flat hairline across the forehead, pronounced upper ears, prominent right nipple, and a pronounced fold in the hem of the robe under the right arm (IMAGE 3).

While displaying an *urna*, large right nipple, and very elaborate treatment of the *sanghati* across the left chest and arm, another 16th-century contemporary seated Buddha is unusual in that the ears are small and close to its body and it is hollow-cast. (IMAGE 5). Most likely the product of a very provincial workshop, it breaks the prohibition against making hollow-cast images; it is virtually unique among later Sri Lankan Buddha images in that respect.

A large standing Buddha is also unusual for this period (IMAGES 6a and 6b). Modeled after the monumental standing Buddha at Avukana, it is unique among images produced during the Period of Divided Kingdoms in that it has a pleated robe that follows the late Anuradhapura period style. Contrary to the treatment of most standing Buddha images of the period, a neatly folded *sanghati* is not depicted draped across the left shoulder. Like the 8th-century image at Avukana, the forms of the body are massive, but more subtly suggested beneath the robe. The right and

Seated Buddha
Divided Kingdoms Period: 16th Century
Bronze, Hollow-cast
H 10cm W 9.1cm
IMAGE 5

left hands are full and fleshy, conveying a sense of power and strength. The head and face however are handled in a very different manner; features of the face are more sharply defined, the mouth is wider, and the form of the chin is broader and more pronounced. The ears stand out more from the side of the head and are more elaborately delineated. The treatment of the hair is quite different from most late Anuradhapura images, as well as those from the Polonnaruva and Divided Kingdoms periods. It is much higher, as if it has been raised in a smooth curve to contain the mass of the *usnisa*, as in the Avukana statue (IMAGE 2, page 69). When viewed from the side (IMAGE 6a) this is even more pronounced, along with the sharp profile of the nose, mouth and chin that are not found in images produced during the preceeding periods, and rarely by artists working during the succeeding period with the capital at Kandy. As this figure is unusually large for a Sri Lankan cast bronze Buddha of any period and the craftsmanship and technical aspects are so fine, it must have been a royal commission. A date during the reign of Parakramabahu VI (1411–1466) at Gampola is tentatively suggested.

Standing Buddha
Divided Kingdoms Period: 15th Century
Gilt Bronze
H 53cm W 15cm
IMAGE 6a (Side view)

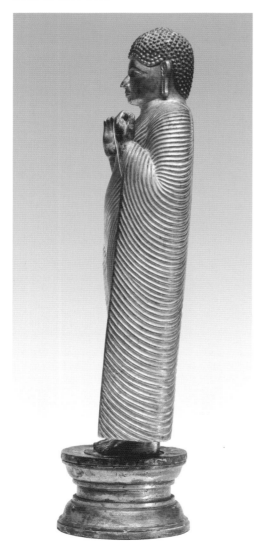

Standing Buddha
Divided Kingdoms Period: 15th Century
Gilt Bronze
H 53cm W 15cm
IMAGE 6b (Front view)

Seated Buddha (Detail of Hands and Feet)
Divided Kingdoms Period: 16th Century
Gilt Bronze
H 52cm W 35.6cm D 20.3cm

Seated Buddha
Divided Kingdoms Period
16th Century
Gilt Bronze
H 52cm W 35.6cm D 20.3cm

Seated Buddha
Divided Kingdoms Period
15th Century
Bronze
H 19.5cm W 16cm D 10cm

Seated Buddha under Makara Torana
Divided Kingdoms Period: 16th Century
Silver
H 20cm W 14cm D 5.8cm

Standing Buddha
Divided Kingdoms Period: 16th Century
Bronze
H 23.5cm   W 7.4cm

Standing Buddha
Divided Kingdoms Period: 15th Century
Bronze
H 24.9cm   W 7.3cm   D 8.7cm

Standing Buddha
Divided Kingdoms Period: 16th–17th Century
Bronze
H 12.5cm W 4cm D 2.7cm

Standing Buddha
Divided Kingdoms Period: 16th Century
Bronze
H 28cm W 9.2cm D 5.6cm

Seated Buddha
Divided Kingdoms Period: 16th Century
Bronze
H 8.2cm   W 6cm   D 3.3cm

Seated Buddha
Divided Kingdoms Period: 16th Century
Bronze
H 8.9cm   W 5.7cm   D 3cm

Seated Buddha
Divided Kingdoms Period: 16th Century
Silver
H 11cm   W 8.8cm   D 4.2cm

Seated Buddha
Divided Kingdoms Period: 16th Century
Bronze, Hollow-cast
H 10cm   W 9.1cm   D 3.6cm

KANDYAN PERIOD

1480–1815

Seated Buddha—Lankatilaka Vihara

Kandyan Period (1480—1815)

John Listopad—Stanford University

The repeated decimations of the Buddhist order at the end of the Period of Divided Kingdoms and early in the Kandyan period resulted in a clear break with previous artistic styles. A new style of Buddha image emerged under the Nayakkar kings of Kandy. It was distinguished by a renewed interest in the aesthetic potential of the pleated robe, most likely inspired by deeply revered ancient Sinhalese monumental images of the late Anuradhapura period like the Buddha at Avukana and the Gal Vihara images at Polonnaruva. The reason for the revival of Buddha images wearing a pleated robe are unclear, but perhaps it was a reaction against the Chola and South Asian styles of depicting the Buddha wearing a thin robe without pleats. All Buddha images made during the 18th- and 19th-centuries are depicted wearing elaborately pleated robes in which all of the pleats move rhythmically in a shimmering zigzag pattern, rather than the sweeping gentle curves composed of parallel lines of the Anuradhapura period. It is as if the Divided Kingdoms Period practice of decorating the hems of the robes and *sanghati* with a few accents was applied to the entire surface of the robe. Despite their elaborate surface treatment of the pleats, Kandyan artists almost always depicted other elements of the robes, such as the *sanghati,* flat. The individual elements of the body and face became increasingly stylized.

Two major stylistic movements evolved during the Kandyan period. One was associated with the court workshops and is characterized by a more elongated face. It is generally associated with images made in brick and stucco in monasteries that Kirti Sri Rajasinha refurbished and large, royally commissioned bronzes (IMAGE 1). Inspired by the hairstyles of the late Anuradhapura period, the hairline across the forehead may incline forward in a widow's peak or incline inwards over the temples in a slightly more exaggerated interpretation of the hairstyle of the monumental Buddha at Avukana.

Several figures in this exhibition belong to this iconographic tradition. Two of them

Standing Buddhas
Kandyan Period: 18th Century
Gilt Bronze
LEFT: H 53cm W 16cm   RIGHT: H 52cm W 14.5cm
IMAGE 1

form an almost identical pair (IMAGE 1). Their large size and the quality of their execution almost certainly designate them as royal commissions, and their closeness in style suggests that they might have been part of an elaborate altar arrangement, perhaps flanking a seated Buddha.[7] In addition to the zigzag pattern of pleats activating the surface of the robe, they are distinguished from Buddha images of the Divided Kingdoms by a larger and broader *sirispata* and less-pronounced right nipple. Another standing image of very fine quality has a slightly rounder face, but still falls within the type (IMAGE 2). As in the Divided Kingdoms, the hem of the *uttarasanga* passes from under the *sanghati*, along the side of the torso and over the left arm, but in a clearer and more pronounced manner. Two seated images also belong to this iconographic tradition (IMAGES 3 and 4). Roughly one-half the height of the standing images, they conform to the same iconometric formula.

There is a great variation in images within this iconometric tradition. A standing Buddha's body is relatively taller and thinner, the waist narrower, and the head and hands are smaller than is typical for this type, resulting in an almost feminine appearing image (IMAGE 5). The treatment of the pleats of the robe are also unusual in that they part left and right from the center and both the lower right edges of the *uttarasanga* and *antaravasaka* project outwards in a sharp

Standing Buddha
Kandyan Period: 18th Century
Gilt Bronze
H 57cm W 15cm
IMAGE 2

Seated Buddha
Kandyan Period: 18th Century
Gilt Bronze with Blue Hardstone Eyes
H 28cm W 23cm D 10cm
IMAGE 3

Seated Buddha
Kandyan Period: 18th Century
Bronze with Lacquered Gilt
H 26cm W 21cm D 12cm
IMAGE 4

point. It seems likely that this treatment was inspired either by a Burmese standing Buddha image or one made during the Period of Divided Kingdoms after a Burmese Buddha image.

The second style is generally associated with smaller bronzes and has a more round countenance, similar to the Buddhas at the Gal Vihara. Though they are occasionally very refined and finely finished, most of these images seem to be the products of provincial workshops. The hairlines usually are the same as those of the royally commissioned images, though a few folk images display the Chola-inspired flat hairline of most Polonnaruva and some Divided Kingdoms figures. The robes are treated in the same manner as the royal images. A standing figure in the exhibition (IMAGE 6) displays the same fine craftsmanship, refinement and attention to detail as bronze images that can be attributed to the royal workshops. The round head places it in this group, along with the lack of the three incised neck rings that are a standard iconographic feature of most Buddha images made during the Anuradhapura and Polonnaruva periods and the royal workshops. The lack of neck rings is also common in many seated figures made with rounded heads according to this non-standard iconometric formula seen in Buddha IMAGES 7 and 8.

The reason for the existence of these two styles has not been recorded. It is possible to theorize that because of King Rajasinha I's (1582-1591) persecution of the Buddhist order and monasteries, most of the traditional texts and artistic guides were destroyed. If this was the case, artists who worked in

Standing Buddha
Kandyan Period: 18th Century
Gilt Bronze
H 43cm W 13.5cm
IMAGE 5

bronze outside of the royal workshops may not have had access to texts and formulated their own iconometry from images that did not conform to the traditions of the *Sariputra*.

Standing Buddha
Kandyan Period: 18th Century
Gilt Bronze
H 30.3cm W 7.9cm D 5.2cm
IMAGE 6

END NOTES

1 The Chinese Pilgrim Xuan Zang (602–664) described a flourishing monastic establishment with over 3,000 monks at the Pallava capital of Kanchipuram.

2 Diran Dohanian, *The Mahayana Buddhist Sculpture of Ceylon*, (New York: Garland Publishing Inc., 1977) 84-94.

3 This gesture is very close to *kataka mudra* and is easy to mistake for it.

4 Douglas Barret, "The Later School of Amaravati and its Influences," in *Studies in Indian Sculpture and Painting*, (London: Pindar Press, 1990), 135.

5 This is not a universal stylistic feature, as many Buddha images continued to be made with the front hairline straight across.

6 Seated Sinhalese Buddha images during the Anuradhapura period were usually intended to sit on a cushion base or throne that was cast separately. Only rarely were they cast seated on a double lotus throne.

7 This particular characteristic is also found on many images from the Period of Divided Kingdoms, as well as the great Buddha at Avukana.

8 Published in Ulrich von Schroeder, *Buddhist Sculptures of Sri Lanka*, (Hong Kong: Visual Dharma Publications, 1990), plate 142A, 462. While several of the images illustrated here display a pronounced fold under the right arm, those with a simple hem under the right arm tight against the body are more common during this period. Virtually all images from the Period of Divided Kingdoms display some type of unique treatment in the hems of the robe. This stylistic attribute is more pronounced during the Period of Divided Kingdoms than during any of the preceeding or following periods.

9 The current *usnisa* and *siraspata* on top of the Avukana image are later additions.

10 Examples of this type of iconography can be seen at many Kandy-period temples such as the Talava Rajamahavihara at Marassana.

Seated Buddha
Kandyan Period: 18th Century
Bronze with Paint
H 34.5cm W 30acm
IMAGE 7

Seated Buddha
Kandyan Period: 18th Century
Gilt Bronze with Paint
H 11.2cm W 9.5cm
IMAGE 8

Standing Buddha
Kandyan Period: 18th Century
Gilt Bronze
H 65cm W 22cm D 22cm

Standing Buddha
Kandyan Period
18th Century
Gilt Bronze
H 65cm W 22cm D 22cm

Standing Buddha
Kandyan Period: 18th Century
Gilt Bronze
H 53cm W 16cm

Standing Buddha
Kandyan Period: 18th Century
Gilt Bronze
H 52cm W 14.5cm

Pair of Standing Buddhas (Pictured individually on pages 140 & 141)
Kandyan Period: 18th Century
Gilt Bronze
LEFT: H 53cm W 16cm D 16cm
RIGHT: H 52cm W 14.5cm D 14.5cm

Standing Buddha
Kandyan Period: 18th Century
Gilt Bronze
H 57cm W 15cm D 15cm

Seated Buddha (Side view)
Kandyan Period: 18th Century
Bronze with Paint
H 34.5cm W 30cm D 18cm

Seated Buddha (Front view)
Kandyan Period
18th Century
Bronze with Paint
H 34.5cm W 30cm D 18cm

Standing Buddha
Kandyan Period: 18th Century
Gilt Bronze
H 48cm W 14cm D 14cm

Standing Buddha
Kandyan Period: 18th Century
Gilt Bronze
H 43cm W 13.5cm D 13.5cm

Seated Buddha
Kandyan Period: 18th Century
Gilt Bronze with Blue Hard Stone Eyes
H 28cm W 23cm D 10cm

Standing Buddha
Kandyan Period: 18th Century
Gilt Bronze
H 30.3cm W 7.9cm D 5.2cm

Seated Buddha
Kandyan Period: 18th Century
Bronze with Lacquered Gilt
H 26cm W 21cm D 12cm

Standing Buddha
Kandyan Period: 18th Century
Gilt Bronze
H 29.5cm W 9.1cm D 4.2cm

Standing Buddha
Kandyan Period: 18th Century
Gilt Bronze
H 39.5cm W 10cm D 5cm

Standing Buddha
Kandyan Period: 18th Century
Gilt Bronze
H 36cm W 11.6cm D 6.8cm

Standing Buddha
Kandyan Period: 18th Century
Gilt Bronze
H 34.6cm W 9.1cm D 7.5cm

Standing Buddha
Kandyan Period: 18th Century
Gilt Bronze
H 33cm W 9.1cm D 9.9cm

Standing Buddha
Kandyan Period: 18th Century
Bronze
H 51.5cm W 12cm D 12cm

Standing Buddha
Kandyan Period: 18th Century
Bronze
H 46cm   W 13cm   D 6.5cm

Standing Buddha
Kandyan Period: 18th Century
Bronze
H 39.5cm   W 13cm   D 8cm

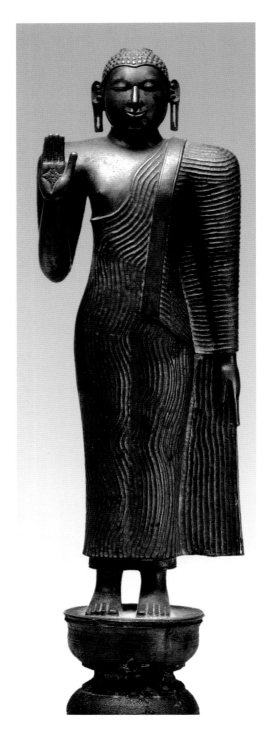 

Standing Buddha
Kandyan Period: 18th Century
Bronze
H 39.5cm w 11.6cm D 7.7cm

Standing Buddha
Kandyan Period: 18th Century
Bronze
H 66cm w 19cm D 19cm

Standing Buddha
Kandyan Period: 18th Century
Bronze
H 70cm W 20cm D 20cm

Standing Buddha
Kandyan Period: 18th Century
Silvered Bronze
H 40cm W 13cm D 13cm

Standing Buddha on Wooden Pedestal
Kandyan Period: 18th Century
Bronze and Wood with Paint
H 46cm W 15.4cm D 9cm

Seated Buddha on Wooden Pedestal
Kandyan Period
18th Century
Bronze and Wood with Paint
H 33cm W 16cm D 6cm

Seated Buddha
Kandyan Period: 18th Century
Gilt Bronze
H 9.8cm W 8.8cm D 4.2cm

Seated Buddha
Kandyan Period: 18th Century
Gilt Bronze
H 12.2cm W 9.3cm D 4cm

Seated Buddha
Kandyan Period: 18th Century
Bronze
H 11.2cm W 9.5cm D 4.5cm

Seated Buddha
Kandyan Period: 18th Century
Gilt Bronze
H 11.8cm W 10.7cm D 4.7cm

Seated Buddha
Kandyan Period: 18th Century
Gilt Bronze
H 22cm W 16cm D 10cm

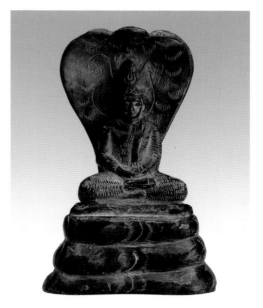

Seated Buddha Beneath Naga-King Mucalinda
Kandyan Period: 18th Century
Bronze
H 15.4cm W 9.8cm D 4cm

Seated Buddha
Kandyan Period: 18th Century
Silver, Hollow-cast
H 9.7cm W 10cm D 4cm

Standing Bodhistattva
Kandyan Period: 18th–19th Century
Bronze
H 14.6cm W 4.2cm D 3.7cm

Seated Buddha
Kandyan Period
18th Century
Plaster and Wood with Paint
H 84cm W 55cm D 39cm

Standing Buddha
Kandyan Period: 18th Century
Ivory
H 32.5cm   W 8.6cm   D 9cm

Standing Buddha on Wooden Pedestal under Ivory Makara Torana
Kandyan Period: 18th Century
Ivory
H 84cm W 36cm D 17cm

Standing Buddha on Wooden Pedestal under Ivory Makara Torana (Detail of *Kirtimukha*)
Kandyan Period: 18th Century
Ivory
H 84cm W 36cm D 17cm

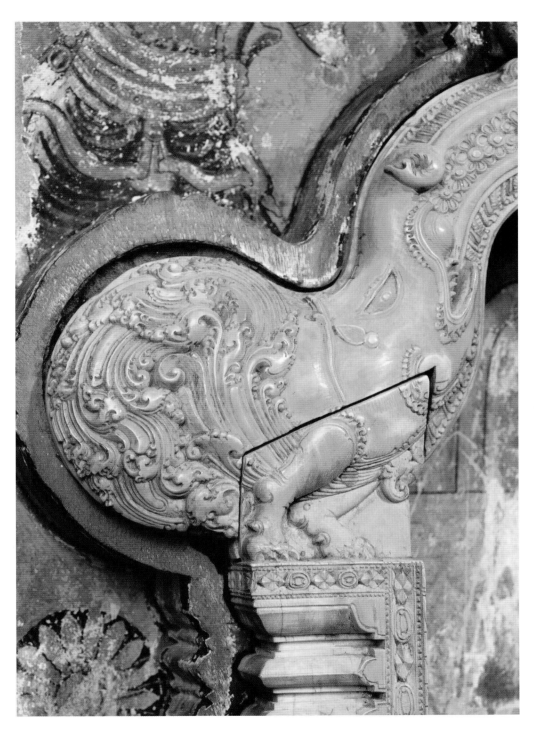

Standing Buddha on Wooden Pedestal under Ivory Makara Torana (Detail of *Makara*)
Kandyan Period: 18th Century
Ivory
H 84cm W 36cm D 17cm

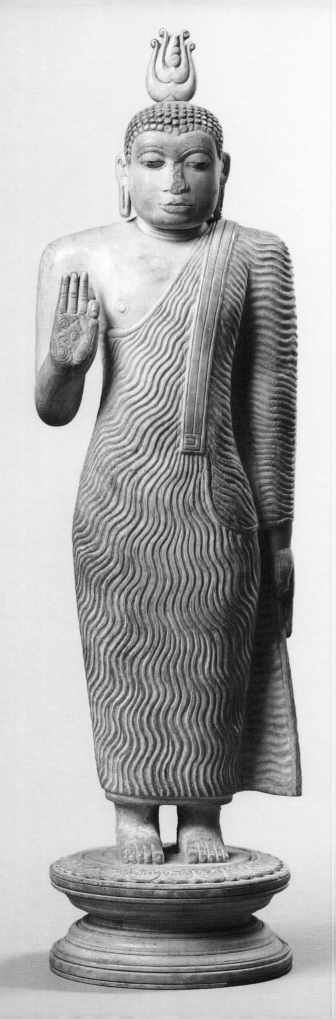

Standing Buddha
Kandyan Period
18th Century
Ivory
H 31.8cm W 8.6cm D 7.8cm

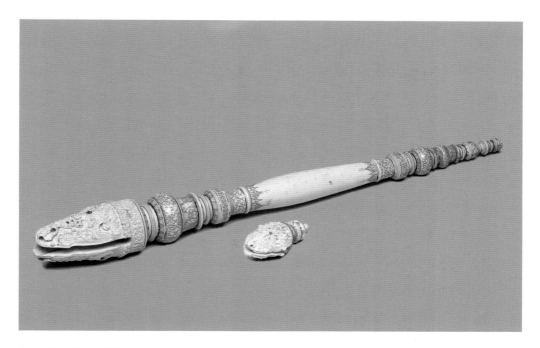

Fan Handle and Finial
Kandyan Period: 18th Century
Ivory
H 49cm W 5.5cm D 5.5cm
FINIAL H 8.6cm W 4cm D 3cm

THE BUDDHA'S
FOOTPRINT

Buddhapada in Kandyan Style
Kandyan Period: 19th Century

The Buddha's Footprint

Sherry Montgomery—Phoenix Art Museum

Sri Lanka's 5th-century chronicle, the *Mahavamsa*, opens with an account of Sakyamuni Buddha's three miraculous visits to the ancient island of Lanka and a description of the origin of one of the island's most revered relics, the footprint on Mt. Sumanakuta. Following the forty-nine days after his enlightenment, the Buddha resolved to preach the *dharma* to all who would receive him. In his omniscience, he foresaw in Lanka a great nation "where his doctrine would shine in glory" and he arose in the air and flew to the island.[1] On his third and final visit, he miraculously ascended Mt. Sumanakuta (Adam's Peak), where he left his footprint in a large stone.[2] The depression, measuring one-meter by one-half meter, has been revered for centuries and remains Sri Lanka's most frequented pilgrimage site. Sri Lanka is not unique in having been honored by the Buddha in this manner. Other countries have similar tales of miraculous visits and footprints *(buddha-padas)* have been venerated in places as far west as Afghanistan, as far east as Japan, and as far south as the Malay Peninsula. Although *buddhapadas* take on local characteristics wherever they are found, they remain essentially a manifest form of the Buddha and an object of worship.

Footprints emerged as a symbol of the Buddha very early in the history of Buddhist art. The earliest surviving examples are found in India and date from the 2nd-century B.C. They appear most frequently in stone reliefs, either as part of a narrative scheme or in isolation, and in rock and wall paintings on early Buddhist architecture. They have survived in paintings on cloth and in manuscript form more rarely, perhaps due to the fragile nature of these media. Generally associated with the veneration of relics and the *stupas* that encase them, *buddhapadas* appeared on reliefs that adorned the fences, gates and pillars of the great *stupas*, such as Sanchi, Amaravati and Nagarjunakonda. Long before the appearance of the Buddha figure, artists used symbols to record the Buddha's history and to make him manifest to the pilgrim worshipper. Chinese monks who traveled to India in search of Buddhist scriptures in the first centuries A.D. record examples of isolated *buddhapadas*. These stone depressions were accorded miraculous origins, treated as relics and sometimes encased in a *stupa*. Textual and archaeological evidence reveal that carved footprints, oriented to face the viewer, were located at the eastern and western entrances of *stupas* such as Pataliputra and Amaravati. Like the miraculous *buddhapadas* that inspired them, they functioned as potent mediators of the Buddha's presence and were often strewn with flower offerings.

The cult of relics, including the Holy Footprint (*Sri Pada*), has played a crucial role in the historical development and consolidation of Theravada Buddhism in Sri Lanka.[3] The *Mahavamsa* records two types of Buddha relics: relics the Buddha left behind on his three miraculous visits to the island, and others brought from India under the protection of Sri Lankan kings. Distributed throughout the island, with the greatest number concentrated at the ancient capital of Anuradhapura, they are frequent subjects in Sri Lankan art. The *solosmasthana*, or "sacred places," are sixteen pilgrimage destinations associated with the Buddha's relics that often form a composition in Sri Lankan art. The *solosmasthana* is the subject of a Kandyan period (c. 19th century) manuscript cover in the exhibition (IMAGES 1a, 1b and 1c). *Stupas*, the Mahabodhi tree, and the Reclining Buddha at Polonnaruva are arranged symmetrically in two registers with the Holy Footprint (*Sri Pada*) occupying the central position. The physical presence of these relics in sites scattered throughout the island essentially extends the story of the Buddha's last life to encompass Sinhalese national history and the local concerns of the Sinhalese people.

Buddhapadas are not only a manifestation of the divine presence, but also a distillation of various ways Buddhahood has been envisioned. On the one hand, they are reminders of Shakyamuni Buddha's willingness to forsake his life as a prince to walk the path of a mendicant ascetic and to carry the message of spiritual release to all,

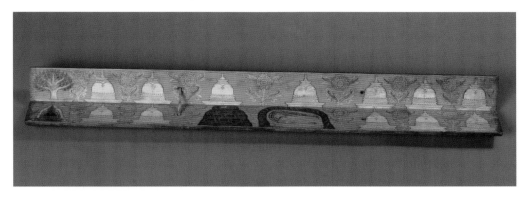

Manuscript Cover
Kandyan Period: 19th Century
Wood with Paint Detail
H 63cm W 6cm
IMAGE 1a

Manuscript Cover Illustrating
Adam's Peak (Detail)
IMAGE 1b

Manuscript Cover Illustrating
Mahiyangana Dagoba (Detail)
IMAGE 1c

Seated Buddha (Detail of hands and feet)
Polonnaruva Period: 12th Century
Gal Vihara
IMAGE 2

regardless of caste. According to the textual and artistic record, *buddhapadas* are also indicators of his transcendent nature for he hovers above the ground, his feet emit rays of light, and blossoming flowers or precious jewels spontaneously appear in his wake.[4] His feet and hands are covered with the auspicious marks (*laksana*) of a perfected being, a *mahapurusa*.[5] Innumerable good deeds performed in previous lives predestined him to take his final birth bearing corporeal signs that would distinguish him as a universal monarch and as a Buddha. The *Lakkhana Sutta* of the *Digha Nikaya*, a part of the Pali Canon of Buddhist scriptures, describes 32 marks, each symbolic of specific acts of merit performed by the Buddha in his past lives. One of these marks, the thousand-spoked wheel, appears on the soles of the Buddha's feet and his hands. Later, the wheel took on additional significance because it represented the Buddha's First Sermon when he "turned the Wheel of the Law" (*dharmacakra*), and laid the foundation for the philosophical system that would become the Buddhist religion. In Sri Lanka, artists often preferred to represent these wheels as flowers, examples of which appear on the feet of the monumental *Seated Buddha* at Gal Vihara at Polonnaruva (c.12th century) (IMAGE 2) and on the *buddhapadas* at Isuramuniya, of the Anuradhapura period (IMAGE 3).

Several Buddha images in this exhibition display lotus marks on hands and feet, but it is the rare, late Kandyan period (c.1480-1815) painting on cloth that most

Footprints of the Buddha
Anuradhapura Period: 3rd Century
IMAGE 3

exuberantly illustrates this stylistic prefer-
ence (IMAGE 4). The footprint is embellished
with a variety of flowers, including red and
white water lilies, red, white and golden
lotuses, and red and yellow jasmine. The
golden lotus in the center of the sole is
surrounded by trefoil palmettes (*nandyavarta*)
and has a center resembling a spoked
wheel, reinforced by the large, red flower
on the heel with its whirling center (*cakra
padma*). Both are reminicent of *dharma-*

cakra. Luminosity is indicated by the undulating aureole that surrounds the footprint
and encompasses the attendant worship-
pers. The Buddha, symbolized by his
footprint, hovers over a double lotus throne
embellished with flower offerings. The footprint faces the viewer in keeping with the
orientation of stone *buddhapadas,* under-
scoring its iconic status. The throne is
flanked by two figures: a monk and a god.
The monk, perhaps the donor of the

Buddhapada in Kandyan Style
Kandyan Period: 19th Century
Painting on Cloth
H 207cm W 95cm D 00cm
IMAGE 4

royal ease with hands raised in worship, may represent Sakka (Indra), the model of Buddhist kingship and patronage.[6] This hieratic, monumental style is typical of late Kandyan painting as is the restricted palette and use of bold, primary colors such as cinnabar red, yellow, and black. Two-dimensionality and reliance on line to heighten visual interest is also character-istic of mural paintings that blanket the interior spaces of rock and built shrines in Sri Lanka.[7] It is possible that the painting was used in outdoor liturgy or hung in a temporary pavilion for ritual occasions like births, marriages or deaths. Given the hier-atic arrangement, similar to images of the Buddha figure flanked by attendants, it was most likely an object of veneration that was more portable than a sculpted image.

The notion of the Buddha as superior to a *cakravartin* is an important component in the creation and veneration of footprint imagery. The painting featured in this exhi-bition is emblematic of the ideal Buddhist world order put forth in the *Mahavamsa*. The chronicle describes the forging of Sri

painting, holds two lotuses, respectfully raised to his forehead prior to placing them on the flower altar in front of the footprint (IMAGE 5). The god, seated in a position of

Lanka into a Buddhist nation. The universal power of the Buddha and his teachings are pitted against the limited power of local gods and human beings. The ideal is ultimately achieved by the creation of a reciprocal relationship between the Sinhalese ecclesia and the monarchy. The king must set an example for the people and look after the welfare of the monastic community. He must ensure its well-being and prosperity through military protection and material generosity. In so doing, he becomes like Sakka, the king of the gods, who serves the Buddha and strives for personal enlightenment. In turn, the Sinhalese monastic community (*sangha*) cares for the relics, preserves the true Buddhist doctrine and legitimizes the authority of the king. The painting is a concise representation of this reciprocity and the special position Sri Lanka holds in the preservation and transmission of *dharma* to the rest of the world."

Buddhapada in Kandyan Style
Kandyan Period: 19th Century
Detail of image 4 Painting on Cloth
IMAGE 5

END NOTES

1   Douglas Bullis, trans, *The Mahavamasa: The Great Chronicle of Sri Lanka* (Fremont, CA: Asian Humanities Press, 1999), 47.

2   Mount Sumanakuta is also known as Sri Pada ("Holy Footprint") or Adam's Peak. Located in the island's south-central highlands, the mountain's significance as a pilgrimage site predates the introduction of Buddhism. The ancient name of the mountain is derived from Sumana, one of four guardian deities of the island and the brother of Rama, the hero of the Hindu epic *The Ramayana*. The site is also sacred to Muslims, who believe that Allah put Adam on the mountain after expelling him from Eden.

3   See John Listopad's essay on the cult of relics in this volume.

4   Scriptural accounts of the miraculous powers of the Buddha's feet can be found in J. J. Jones' translation of *The Mahavastu* in *The Mahavastu* (London: Luzac & Company, Ltd. 1949) I, 257, and in J. Auboyer's translation of a passage from the Amitayaurbuddhanusmurti-sutra in "A Note on the Feet and Their Symbolism in Ancient India" in Kusumanjalis. *New Interpretation of Indian Art & Culture*, ed. M. S. Nagaraja Rao (Delhi: Agam, 1987), 125-127.

5   Lotus flowers on the feet are also among the distinctive signs that can number as high as 132. See Anna Maria Quagliotti, *Buddhapadas: An Essay on the Representations of the Footprints of the Buddha with a Descriptive Catalog of the Indian Specimens From the 2nd Century B.C. to the 4th Century A.D.* (Kamakura: Institute of the Silk Road Studies, 1998).

6   Sakka is the Sinhalese version of the Hindu god Indra.

7   A late 18th-century mural depicting Sakka venerating Sri Pada appears at Ridi Vihara and is illustrated in John Clifford Holt, *The Religious World of Kirti Sri: Buddhism, Art and Politics in Late Medieval Sri Lanka,* (New York: Oxford University Press, 1996), 66. The lack of perspective shows clearly as the footprint is tilted up towards the viewer.

BIOGRAPHY

Sherry Montgomery, M.C. is Curatorial Assistant in Asian Art at Phoenix Art Museum. She is a graduate student in Art History with a specialization in Asian art at the School of Art, Katherine K. Herberger College of Fine Arts, Arizona State University. She currently holds the Eirene Peggy Lamb Endowed Scholarship in Art. Previously, she earned a Master's Degree in Counseling from Arizona State University.

BIBLIOGRAPHY
GLOSSARY

Bibliography

Bandaranayake, Senake Dias. *The Rock and Wall Paintings of Sri Lanka* (Colombo: Lake House, 1986).

——. *Sinhalese Monastic Architecture: The Viharas of Anuradhapura* (Leiden: E. J. Brill, 1974).

Barrett, Douglas "The Later School of Amaravati and its Influences," (published 1954) reprinted in *Studies in Indian Sculpture and Painting* (London: Pindar Press, 1990) 128-147.

Berchert, Heinz ed. *Buddhism in Ceylon and Studies on Religious Syncretism in Buddhist Countries: Report on a Symposium in Gottingen* (Gottingen: Vendenhoeck & Ruprecht, 1978).

Boisselier, Jean, *Archaeologia Mundi: Ceylon* (Geneva: Nagel Publishers, 1979).

Chulavamsa, trans. W. Geiger, 2 vols. (Colombo: Ceylon Government Information Department, 1953).

Coomaraswamy, Ananda K. *Medieval Sinhalese Art*, 2nd ed. (New York, Pantheon Books, 1956).

——. *Bronzes from Ceylon, Chiefly in the Colombo Museum, Memoirs of the Colombo Museum, Series A, No. 1*, reprint of 1914 ed. (Colombo: Department of Government Printing, Sri Lanka, 1978).

Digha Nikaya, Maurice Walshe, trans. as *The Long Discourses of the Buddha: A Translation of the Digha Nikaya* (Boston: Wisdom Publications, 1995).

Dohanian, Diran Kavork. *The Mahayana Buddhist Sculpture of Ceylon*, reprint of 1964 ed. (New York: Garland Publishing, 1977).

Epigraphia Zeylanica – Being lithic and other inscriptions of Ceylon
    Vol. I (1904-1912) ed. Don Martin de Zilva Wikremasinghe, reprint of 1912 ed. (Colombo, Aitken Spence and Company, ltd., 1976).
    Vol. II (1912-1927) ed. Don Martin de Zilva Wikremasinghe, reprint of 1928 ed. (Colombo, Government Press, 1985).

Gangoly, O. C. *South Indian Bronzes*, (Calcutta, 1978).

Gatellier, Marie. *Peintures Murales du Sri Lanka: école kandyenne XVIII-XIX siécles*, 2 Vols. (Paris: Publications de l'école francaise d'éxtreme-orient, 1991).

Geiger, Wilhelm. *The Culture of Ceylon in Medieval Times*, ed. H. Bechert (Wiesbaden: Otto Harrassowitz, 1960).

Godakumbara, C. E. *The Kotavehera at Dedigama, Memoirs of the Archaeological Survey of Ceylon*, Vol. VII (Colombo: Department of Archaeology, 1969).

Gombrich, Richard F. "The Consecration of a Buddha Image," *Journal of Asian Studies*, Vol. XXVI (1996), No. 1, 23-36.

——. "The Buddha's Eye, The Evil Eye and Dr. Ruelius," *Buddhism in Ceylon and Studies on Religious Syncretism in Buddhist Countries*, ed. Heinz Bechert (1978), 335-338.

Holt, John Clifford. *The Religious World of Kirti Sri: Buddhism, Art, and Politics in Late Medieval Sri Lanka*, (New York: Oxford University Press, 1996).

Knox, Robert. *An Historical Relation of Ceylon*, reprint of 1681 edition (Glasgow: University Press, 1911).

Mahavamsa, trans. W. Geiger (Colombo, 1950). Mudiyanse, Nadasena. *The Art and Architecture of the Gampola Period, 1341-1425 A.D.* (Columbia: M.D. Gunasena, 1963).

Paranavitana, Senarat. *The Stupa in Ceylon, Memoirs of the Archeological Survey of Ceylon*, Vol. V, reprint of 1946 ed. (Colombo: State Printing Corporation, 1980).

——. *Art and Architecture of Ceylon: Polonnaruva Period*, (Columbo: Arts Council of Ceylon, 1954).

Rahula, Walpola. *History of Buddhism in Ceylon: The Anuradhapura Period* (Colombo: M. D. Gunasena & Co., Ltd., 1966).

Ruelius, Hans. *Sariputra and Alekyalaksana*, (Gottingen: Dissertation Georg-August Universitat, 1974).

——. "Netrapratisthápana – eine singhalesische Zeremonie zür Weihe von Kultbildern," *Buddhism in Ceylon and Studies on Religious Syncretism in Buddhist Countries*, ed. Heinz Bechert. (1978), 304-334.

Snellgrove, David L. (general editor). *The Image of the Buddha*, (Paris, 1978).

Stevenson, Sinclair. *The Rites of the Twice-Born*, reprint of 1920 edition (Delhi: Oriental Books Reprint Corporation, 1971).

Vacissara, Thera. *The Chronicle of the Thupa and the Thupavamsa*, transl. N. A. Jayawickrama (London: Luzac & Company, ltd., 1971).

The Vastuvidya Sastra ascribed to Manjusri, E. W. Marasinghe trans., (Delhi, Sri Satguru Publications, 1989)

von Schoreder, Ulrich. *Buddhist Sculptures of Sri Lanka*, (Hong Kong: Visual Dharma Publications, 1990).

——. *The Golden Age of Sculpture in Sri Lanka*, (Hong Kong: Visual Dharma Publications, ltd. 1992).

Ward, W. E. "Selected Buddhist Symbols in Sinhalese Decorative Arts," *Artibus Asiae*, Vol. XIII (1950), No. 4, 270-96.

Glossary

abhaya mudra – gesture symbolizing benediction through removing fear. Hand is raised to shoulder height with the arm crooked and the palm of the hand facing outwards.

ahuyavarada mudra – gesture of "inviting and giving." The hand is held raised and almost closed. Similar to k*ataka mudra.*

anda – the dome of a *dagaba* or *stupa.*

antaravasaka – the lower robe worn by a Buddhist monk.

asis mudra – a variant of *abhaya mudra* in which the hand is turned to the image's left. This gesture is unique to Sri Lanka.

Bodhi Tree – the tree under which the Buddha attained enlightenment.

Buddhacaitya – reminder of the Buddha.

buddhapada – footprint of a Buddha; used as a symbol of the Buddha.

cakra – wheel or discus. In Buddhism, the cakra refers to the turning of the "wheel of the law."

cakravartin – universal monarch.

Chola dynasty – a South Indian dynasty that ruled from mid 9th to 14th-century

Chulavamsa, "the Lessor Lineage." The history of the reigns of the kings of Sri Lanka from Sirimeghavanna (363–390) to Sirivikkamarajasina (1798–1815).

dagaba – Sinhalese word for *stupa*. A reliquary mound.

danda – ritual staff.

dharma – the Buddhist Law or teachings. One of the three jewels of Buddhism, including the Buddha and the Buddhist monastic order, the *Sangha.* Buddhist philosophy recognizes the Buddha as a manifestation of the cosmic law that underlies the universe.

dharmacakra – "Wheel of the Law;" stylized representation of a spoked wheel often used to symbolize the Buddha's First Sermon. The Buddha's first sermon is said to have set "the wheel of the law" into motion.

dharmacaitya – "doctrinal reminders." The teachings of the Buddha or literature on it.

dhatucaitya – physical relics of the Buddha or the monument that contains them.

dhyana mudra – gesture of meditation. The left hand rests palm up on the lap, the right hand is placed palm up on top of it.

Garbha vidhana – "literally impregnation of the womb," the ritual consecration of a site.

Gupta dynasty – a central Indian dynasty that ruled from the 4th to 6th-century.

karanduvas – reliquary containers.

kataka mudra – the gesture of holding an object.

kirtimukha – "face of the devourer." The kirtimukha often lacks a lower jaw. Often used atop gateways to temples, *torana*, or as a type of framing device. Common to both South Indian Buddhist and Hindu iconography.

laksana (Pali – lakkana) – special marks or characteristics.

lokapalas – guardian deities of the four directions.

mahapurusa – the universal man.

Mahavamsa – "the Great Lineage." The history of the kings of Sri Lanka to the reign of

Mahayana Buddhism – "The Great Vehicle." Considered to be unorthodox by Theravada Buddhists, it stresses the Bodhisattva ideal and the concept of universal salvation.

makara – a mythical aquatic creature.

makara torana – a gateway form often used as a framing device for Buddha images.

navandanno – the caste of smiths.

nandyavarta – a floral or foliate motif characterized by three lanceolate petals or leaves and associated with early Buddhist imagery. It is also referred to as the *triratna* or three jewels symbolizing the three parts of the Buddhist religion: The Buddha, his teachings and the Buddhist monastic order, the *sangha*.

Nayak dynasty – ruled from their court at Madurai in South India from the late 16th-century to the early 18th-century. During the Kandy period, Nayak princes were invited to ascend the throne of Sri Lanka.

nekata – an asterism of the moon.

netra pinkama – a consecration ceremony "opening the eyes" of an image.

netra pratisthanapana utsavaya – "the festival of the setting of the eyes," a consecration ceremony.

padma – lotus flower, symbol of purity and transcendence.

Pallava dynasty – a South Indian dynasty that flourished from the early 7th-century to the late 9th-century.

paribhogacaitya – "reminder by association." Objects that were used by the Buddha or associated with events in his life.

samadhi mudra – see *dhyana mudra*.

sanghati – the shawl worn by a Buddhist monk.

shanka – conch shell.

Sariputra – a Sinhalese iconographic and iconometric text believed to have been composed during the 12th century. It is derived from the South Indian *silpasastra* tradition.

silpasastra – text giving the iconographic and iconometric criteria for making a religious image.

sirispata – the flame ornament on top of the *usnisa* of a Buddha image.

sittaru – sub-cast of smiths that includes image-makers.

sruk – Ladle for pouring liquid offerings during ritual sacrifice.

stupa – a reliquary mound.

Theravada – "Lineage of the Elders." The orthodox sect of Buddhism.

Tripitaka – "the Three Baskets." The three groups of Theravada Buddhist canonical scriptures: the book of monastic rules, the teachings, and the commentaries on the teachings.

uddesikacaitya – "indicative reminders or symbols." Places associated with events in the life of the Buddha, copies of the famous relics of the Buddha, copies of *paribhogacetiya*, and Buddha images.

urna – swirl or tuft of hair between the eyebrows. One of the 32 principle *lakkana*.

usnisa – a cranial protuberance, literally a "royal turban." Considered to be one of the *lakkana* of the Buddha.

uttarasanga – the outer robe worn by a Buddhist monk.

Vajrayana Buddhism – "the Adamantine or Diamond Vehicle." Esoteric Buddhism, considered to be heterodox by Theravada Buddhists.

varada mudra – gesture symbolizing offering, charity and compassion. The arm is lowered with the hand open and the palm facing out.

vinaya – the book of discipline and rules of monastic behavior. One of the three parts of the *tripitika*.

virasana – seated posture where one foot rests on the ground and the other leg is folded so that its foot rests on the calf of the other leg.

vitarka mudra – gesture symbolizing elucidation, discussion or argument. The thumb and the forefinger touch.